# 50 Recipes for Vietnamese Street Eats at Home

By: Kelly Johnson

# Table of Contents

- Pho Bo (Beef Pho)
- Banh Mi Thit Nuong (Grilled Pork Banh Mi)
- Goi Cuon (Spring Rolls)
- Bun Cha (Grilled Pork Vermicelli)
- Com tam suon nuong (Broken Rice with Grilled Pork Chop)
- Banh Xeo (Vietnamese Pancakes)
- Bo Kho (Vietnamese Beef Stew)
- Mi Quang (Quang Style Noodles)
- Bun Thit Nuong Cha Gio (Grilled Pork Noodles with Spring Rolls)
- Banh Canh Cua (Crab Noodle Soup)
- Ca Kho To (Braised Fish in Clay Pot)
- Nom Hoa Chuoi (Banana Flower Salad)
- Canh Chua Ca (Sour Fish Soup)
- Cha Ca Thang Long (Hanoi Turmeric Fish with Dill)
- Bun Rieu Cua (Crab Noodle Soup)
- Xoi Xeo (Sticky Rice with Mung Beans and Fried Shallots)
- Banh Trang Nuong (Grilled Rice Paper with Toppings)
- Che Ba Mau (Three-Color Dessert)
- Bun Bo Hue (Spicy Beef Noodle Soup)
- Ca Phe Sua Da (Vietnamese Iced Coffee)
- Nem Nuong Cuon (Grilled Pork Spring Rolls)
- Chao Long (Rice Porridge with Pork Offal)
- Banh Da Lon (Pandan Layer Cake)
- Goi Du Du Kho Bo (Green Papaya Salad with Beef Jerky)
- Mien Ga (Chicken Glass Noodle Soup)
- Xoi Man (Sweet Sticky Rice with Toppings)
- Cha Tom (Grilled Shrimp on Sugar Cane)
- Nom Oi (Pomelo Salad)
- Bun Oc (Snail Noodle Soup)
- Hu Tieu Nam Vang (Cambodian-Style Noodle Soup)
- Goi Ngo Sen (Lotus Stem Salad)
- Chao Tom Cuon (Shrimp Paste on Sugarcane Skewers)
- Banh Chung (Traditional Tet Sticky Rice Cake)
- Bun Mang Vit (Duck and Bamboo Shoot Noodle Soup)
- Xoi Gac (Red Sticky Rice)

- Goi Ca Trich (Jellyfish Salad)
- Banh Cuon (Steamed Rice Rolls)
- Oc Len Xao Dua (Stir-Fried Snails with Coconut Milk)
- Nom Hoa Chuoi Xanh (Green Banana Flower Salad)
- Bun Oc (Escargot Noodle Soup)
- Che Troi Nuoc (Glutinous Rice Balls in Ginger Syrup)
- Banh Cam (Orange Sesame Balls)
- Lau Ca Keo (Basa Fish Hot Pot)
- Che Ba Ba (Tapioca and Coconut Milk Dessert)
- Banh It Tran (Sticky Rice Dumplings)
- Bun Mang Vit (Duck and Bamboo Shoot Noodle Soup)
- Goi Ngo Sen (Lotus Stem Salad)
- Cha Ca La Vong (Hanoi Turmeric Fish with Dill)
- Muc Nuong Sa Ot (Grilled Lemongrass Squid)
- Che Bap (Corn Pudding)

## Pho Bo (Beef Pho)

*Ingredients:*

- 1 lb (450g) beef sirloin or flank, thinly sliced
- 1 lb (450g) beef brisket or bone marrow
- 8 cups (1.9 liters) beef broth
- 1 package (400g) flat rice noodles (banh pho)
- 1 onion, sliced
- 3-4 slices of ginger
- 3-4 star anise
- 3-4 whole cloves
- 1 cinnamon stick
- 2 tablespoons fish sauce
- 1 tablespoon sugar
- Salt, to taste
- Fresh herbs (cilantro, Thai basil, mint)
- Bean sprouts
- Lime wedges
- Red chili, sliced (optional)
- Hoisin sauce and Sriracha (optional, for serving)

*Instructions:*

Prepare the Broth:
- In a large pot, char the onion and ginger over an open flame or under the broiler for a few minutes until fragrant.
- Add beef brisket or bone marrow to the pot and cover with water. Bring to a boil, then reduce heat and simmer for at least 1 hour, skimming any impurities that rise to the surface.

Toast Spices:
- In a dry pan, toast star anise, cloves, and cinnamon until fragrant. Add them to the broth.

Season the Broth:
- Add fish sauce, sugar, and salt to the broth. Adjust seasoning to taste.

Prepare Rice Noodles:
- Cook rice noodles according to package instructions. Drain and set aside.

Assemble Bowls:

- Arrange a handful of rice noodles and raw beef slices in each serving bowl.

Pour Hot Broth:
- Pour hot broth over the noodles and beef. The hot broth will cook the raw beef slices.

Serve:
- Serve immediately with fresh herbs, bean sprouts, lime wedges, and sliced chili on the side.

Optional:
- Customize your pho with hoisin sauce and Sriracha to taste.

Enjoy:
- Stir the noodles and beef in the hot broth, garnish with herbs, squeeze lime, and savor the deliciousness of homemade Pho Bo!

**Banh Mi Thit Nuong (Grilled Pork Banh Mi)**

*Ingredients:*

*For the Grilled Pork:*

- 1 lb (450g) pork shoulder or pork loin, thinly sliced
- 3 tablespoons soy sauce
- 2 tablespoons fish sauce
- 2 tablespoons honey or sugar
- 2 cloves garlic, minced
- 1 tablespoon vegetable oil
- 1 teaspoon five-spice powder (optional)
- Freshly ground black pepper, to taste

*For the Pickled Vegetables:*

- 1 large carrot, julienned
- 1 daikon radish, julienned
- 1/2 cup rice vinegar
- 1/4 cup sugar
- 1 teaspoon salt

*For the Banh Mi:*

- Baguettes or Vietnamese sandwich rolls
- Mayonnaise
- Maggi sauce or soy sauce
- Fresh cilantro, chopped
- Jalapeño peppers, thinly sliced
- Cucumber, thinly sliced

*Instructions:*

Grilled Pork:

    Marinate Pork:
- In a bowl, combine soy sauce, fish sauce, honey (or sugar), minced garlic, vegetable oil, five-spice powder (if using), and black pepper.

- Add sliced pork to the marinade, ensuring it's well-coated. Marinate for at least 30 minutes to 2 hours.

Grill Pork:
- Preheat grill or grill pan. Grill the marinated pork slices until fully cooked and slightly caramelized. Set aside.

Pickled Vegetables:

Prepare Pickling Liquid:
- In a bowl, dissolve sugar and salt in rice vinegar.

Pickled Vegetables:
- Place julienned carrot and daikon radish in a jar or bowl.
- Pour the pickling liquid over the vegetables, ensuring they are fully submerged.
- Let it pickle for at least 30 minutes in the refrigerator.

Assembling Banh Mi:

Prepare Bread:
- Slice the baguettes or sandwich rolls lengthwise. If desired, lightly toast them.

Spread Condiments:
- Spread mayonnaise on one side of the bread. Drizzle with Maggi sauce or soy sauce for added flavor.

Assemble Ingredients:
- Arrange grilled pork slices on the bread.
- Top with pickled vegetables, fresh cilantro, jalapeño slices, and cucumber.

Serve:
- Close the sandwich and serve immediately.

Enjoy:
- Sink your teeth into the delicious Banh Mi Thit Nuong, savoring the perfect blend of grilled pork, pickled veggies, and flavorful condiments!

**Goi Cuon (Spring Rolls)**

*Ingredients:*

*For the Spring Rolls:*

- Rice paper sheets (banh trang)
- 1 lb (450g) shrimp, peeled, deveined, and cooked
- Rice vermicelli noodles, cooked and cooled
- Lettuce leaves
- Fresh mint leaves
- Fresh cilantro leaves
- Bean sprouts

*For the Dipping Sauce:*

- 1/4 cup hoisin sauce
- 2 tablespoons peanut butter
- 2 tablespoons soy sauce
- 1 tablespoon lime juice
- 1 tablespoon water
- 1 teaspoon Sriracha sauce (optional)

*Instructions:*

Prepare Ingredients:

Cook Shrimp:
- Bring a pot of water to a boil. Add shrimp and cook for 2-3 minutes until they turn pink. Drain, cool, and slice each shrimp in half lengthwise.

Cook Vermicelli Noodles:
- Cook rice vermicelli noodles according to package instructions. Drain and let them cool.

Dipping Sauce:

Prepare Dipping Sauce:

- In a bowl, whisk together hoisin sauce, peanut butter, soy sauce, lime juice, water, and Sriracha (if using). Adjust the consistency with more water if needed.

Assemble Spring Rolls:

Soak Rice Paper:
- Fill a shallow dish with warm water. Dip each rice paper sheet into the water for a few seconds until it becomes pliable.

Arrange Ingredients:
- Lay the softened rice paper on a clean surface.
- On one edge, place a few slices of shrimp, a handful of rice vermicelli, lettuce leaves, mint leaves, cilantro leaves, and bean sprouts.

Roll Spring Rolls:
- Fold the sides of the rice paper over the filling, then tightly roll from the bottom to the top, sealing the edges.

Repeat:
- Repeat the process with the remaining ingredients.

Serve:
- Serve the spring rolls immediately or cover them with a damp cloth to prevent drying.

Enjoy:
- Dip the Goi Cuon in the prepared dipping sauce and enjoy the refreshing taste of these delicious Vietnamese spring rolls!

**Bun Cha (Grilled Pork Vermicelli)**

*Ingredients:*

*For the Grilled Pork:*

- 1 lb (450g) pork shoulder or pork belly, thinly sliced
- 3 tablespoons fish sauce
- 2 tablespoons soy sauce
- 2 tablespoons honey or sugar
- 3 cloves garlic, minced
- 1 tablespoon vegetable oil
- Freshly ground black pepper, to taste

*For the Nuoc Cham (Dipping Sauce):*

- 3 tablespoons fish sauce
- 2 tablespoons rice vinegar
- 2 tablespoons sugar
- 1/2 cup water
- 2 cloves garlic, minced
- 1 red chili, thinly sliced (optional)

*For the Vermicelli Bowl:*

- Rice vermicelli noodles, cooked and cooled
- Lettuce leaves
- Fresh herbs (mint, cilantro)
- Bean sprouts
- Sliced cucumber

*For Garnish:*

- Crushed peanuts
- Fried shallots
- Lime wedges

*Instructions:*

Grilled Pork:

Marinate Pork:
- In a bowl, mix fish sauce, soy sauce, honey (or sugar), minced garlic, vegetable oil, and black pepper.
- Add sliced pork to the marinade, ensuring it's well-coated. Marinate for at least 30 minutes to 2 hours.

Grill Pork:
- Preheat grill or grill pan. Grill the marinated pork slices until fully cooked and slightly caramelized. Set aside.

Nuoc Cham (Dipping Sauce):

Prepare Dipping Sauce:
- In a bowl, combine fish sauce, rice vinegar, sugar, water, minced garlic, and sliced red chili (if using). Stir until sugar dissolves.

Vermicelli Bowl:

Prepare Ingredients:
- Arrange cooked and cooled vermicelli noodles, lettuce leaves, fresh herbs, bean sprouts, and sliced cucumber in individual serving bowls.

Assemble Bowl:
- Top each bowl with the grilled pork slices.

Garnish:
- Sprinkle crushed peanuts and fried shallots over the bowls.

Serve:
- Serve the Bun Cha bowls with lime wedges and the prepared Nuoc Cham on the side.

Enjoy:
- Mix the ingredients in the bowl, drizzle with Nuoc Cham, and savor the delightful combination of grilled pork and fresh, vibrant flavors!

**Com tam suon nuong (Broken Rice with Grilled Pork Chop)**

*Ingredients:*

*For the Grilled Pork Chop:*

- 4 pork chops
- 3 tablespoons soy sauce
- 2 tablespoons fish sauce
- 2 tablespoons honey or sugar
- 3 cloves garlic, minced
- 1 tablespoon vegetable oil
- Freshly ground black pepper, to taste

*For the Broken Rice:*

- 2 cups broken rice (com tam rice)
- Water for rinsing and cooking
- 1 tablespoon vegetable oil
- 1 teaspoon salt

*For the Accompaniments:*

- Pickled vegetables (carrots, daikon)
- Lettuce leaves
- Sliced cucumber
- Fresh herbs (mint, cilantro)
- Lime wedges

*For the Nuoc Cham (Dipping Sauce):*

- 3 tablespoons fish sauce
- 2 tablespoons rice vinegar
- 2 tablespoons sugar
- 1/2 cup water
- 2 cloves garlic, minced
- 1 red chili, thinly sliced (optional)

*Instructions:*

## Grilled Pork Chop:

### Marinate Pork Chop:
- In a bowl, mix soy sauce, fish sauce, honey (or sugar), minced garlic, vegetable oil, and black pepper.
- Coat the pork chops with the marinade and let them marinate for at least 30 minutes to 2 hours.

### Grill Pork Chop:
- Preheat grill or grill pan. Grill the marinated pork chops until fully cooked and slightly caramelized. Set aside.

## Broken Rice:

### Prepare Broken Rice:
- Rinse the broken rice in cold water until the water runs clear.
- In a pot, bring water to a boil. Add the rinsed broken rice, vegetable oil, and salt. Cook until the rice is tender but still slightly chewy. Drain any excess water.

## Nuoc Cham (Dipping Sauce):

### Prepare Dipping Sauce:
- In a bowl, combine fish sauce, rice vinegar, sugar, water, minced garlic, and sliced red chili (if using). Stir until sugar dissolves.

## Assemble Com Tam Suon Nuong:

### Arrange Components:
- Divide the cooked broken rice among serving plates. Top each plate with a grilled pork chop.

### Add Accompaniments:
- Arrange pickled vegetables, lettuce leaves, sliced cucumber, and fresh herbs around the pork chop.

### Garnish:
- Garnish the plate with lime wedges.

### Serve:
- Serve Com Tam Suon Nuong with Nuoc Cham on the side.

### Enjoy:

- Mix the broken rice with the grilled pork chop, add the fresh accompaniments, and drizzle with Nuoc Cham. Enjoy this classic Vietnamese dish with a burst of flavors and textures!

**Banh Xeo (Vietnamese Pancakes)**

*Ingredients:*

*For the Pancake Batter:*

- 1 cup rice flour
- 1 cup coconut milk
- 3/4 cup water
- 1/2 teaspoon turmeric powder
- 1/2 teaspoon salt
- 1/2 teaspoon sugar
- 2 green onions, thinly sliced
- 1/2 lb (225g) pork belly, thinly sliced (optional)
- 1/2 lb (225g) medium-sized shrimp, peeled and deveined
- Bean sprouts
- Fresh herbs (cilantro, mint)

*For the Dipping Sauce (Nuoc Cham):*

- 3 tablespoons fish sauce
- 2 tablespoons rice vinegar
- 2 tablespoons sugar
- 1/2 cup water
- 1 clove garlic, minced
- 1 red chili, thinly sliced (optional)

*For Serving:*

- Lettuce leaves
- Rice paper (optional)
- Mint leaves

*Instructions:*

Pancake Batter:

Prepare Batter:
- In a bowl, whisk together rice flour, coconut milk, water, turmeric powder, salt, and sugar until smooth.
- Add sliced green onions to the batter.

Rest Batter:
- Let the batter rest for at least 30 minutes.

## Dipping Sauce (Nuoc Cham):

Prepare Dipping Sauce:
- In a bowl, combine fish sauce, rice vinegar, sugar, water, minced garlic, and sliced red chili (if using). Stir until sugar dissolves.

## Cooking Banh Xeo:

Heat Pan:
- Heat a non-stick skillet or crepe pan over medium-high heat.

Add Filling:
- If using pork, add thinly sliced pork belly to the pan and cook until browned. Add shrimp and cook until they turn pink.

Pour Batter:
- Pour a ladle of the batter into the pan, swirling it to coat the bottom evenly.

Cook Pancake:
- Allow the pancake to cook until the edges become crispy and golden brown.

Add Bean Sprouts:
- Add a handful of bean sprouts to one half of the pancake.

Fold Pancake:
- Gently fold the pancake in half, covering the bean sprouts.

Serve:
- Transfer the Banh Xeo to a serving plate. Repeat the process with the remaining batter.

## To Serve:

Serve with Lettuce:
- Serve Banh Xeo with lettuce leaves on the side.

Optional Rice Paper:

- Optionally, you can wrap Banh Xeo in rice paper along with fresh herbs like mint leaves.

Dip and Enjoy:
- Dip the Banh Xeo in the Nuoc Cham dipping sauce and enjoy the crispy, flavorful Vietnamese pancakes!

## Bo Kho (Vietnamese Beef Stew)

*Ingredients:*

- 2 lbs (900g) beef stew meat, cut into chunks
- 2 tablespoons vegetable oil
- 1 large onion, thinly sliced
- 3 cloves garlic, minced
- 1 tablespoon ginger, grated
- 2 tablespoons tomato paste
- 3 tablespoons soy sauce
- 2 tablespoons fish sauce
- 1 tablespoon sugar
- 1 tablespoon curry powder
- 1 teaspoon five-spice powder
- 1 teaspoon paprika
- 1 teaspoon ground coriander
- 4 cups beef broth
- 2 cups coconut water
- 3-4 carrots, peeled and sliced into chunks
- 2-3 potatoes, peeled and cubed
- 2-3 stalks lemongrass, bruised
- 3-4 kaffir lime leaves
- Salt and pepper, to taste
- Fresh cilantro and red chili slices for garnish

*Instructions:*

Brown the Beef:
- Heat vegetable oil in a large pot over medium-high heat. Brown the beef chunks in batches until all sides are seared. Remove and set aside.

Aromatics:
- In the same pot, sauté sliced onions until translucent. Add minced garlic and grated ginger, cooking for an additional minute.

Spices and Tomato Paste:
- Stir in tomato paste, soy sauce, fish sauce, sugar, curry powder, five-spice powder, paprika, and ground coriander. Cook for 2-3 minutes to enhance flavors.

Combine Beef and Broth:
- Return the seared beef to the pot, coating it with the spice mixture. Pour in beef broth and coconut water.

Simmer:
- Add carrots, potatoes, lemongrass, and kaffir lime leaves to the pot. Bring the stew to a boil, then reduce heat to low, cover, and simmer for 2-3 hours or until the beef is tender.

Adjust Seasoning:
- Season the Bo Kho with salt and pepper to taste. Remove lemongrass and kaffir lime leaves.

Serve:
- Ladle the stew into bowls. Garnish with fresh cilantro and sliced red chilies.

Enjoy:
- Serve Bo Kho with French bread, rice noodles, or baguette for a hearty and flavorful Vietnamese beef stew experience.

**Mi Quang (Quang Style Noodles)**

*Ingredients:*

*For the Broth:*

- 1 lb (450g) pork bones or chicken bones
- 1 onion, halved and unpeeled
- 1 knob of ginger, sliced
- 1 cinnamon stick
- 3 star anise
- 3 cloves
- 1 cardamom pod
- 6 cups (1.4 liters) water
- 2 tablespoons fish sauce
- Salt and sugar, to taste

*For the Toppings:*

- 1 lb (450g) shrimp, peeled and deveined
- 1 lb (450g) pork belly, thinly sliced
- 1 pack rice noodles
- 1 bunch scallions, chopped
- Fresh herbs (cilantro, mint, basil)
- Bean sprouts
- Lime wedges
- Crushed peanuts
- Chili flakes (optional)

*For the Turmeric Seasoning:*

- 1 tablespoon ground turmeric
- 1 teaspoon annatto seeds (optional, for color)
- 2 tablespoons vegetable oil

*Instructions:*

**Broth:**

Prepare Broth:
- In a large pot, char the onion and ginger over an open flame or under the broiler for a few minutes until fragrant.
- Add pork or chicken bones, cinnamon stick, star anise, cloves, cardamom, water, fish sauce, salt, and sugar to the pot.
- Simmer for at least 1 hour, skimming any impurities that rise to the surface.

**Turmeric Seasoning:**

Make Turmeric Seasoning:
- In a small saucepan, heat vegetable oil over medium heat.
- Add ground turmeric and annatto seeds (if using). Cook until fragrant and the oil takes on a golden color. Strain and set aside.

**Toppings:**

Prepare Toppings:
- Boil the rice noodles according to package instructions. Drain and set aside.
- Cook the shrimp and pork belly in the broth until fully cooked. Remove and set aside.

**Assembly:**

Assemble Mi Quang:
- In a serving bowl, place a portion of rice noodles.
- Arrange cooked shrimp and pork belly on top of the noodles.

Add Seasoning:
- Drizzle the turmeric seasoning over the noodles and toppings.

Pour Broth:
- Ladle the hot broth over the noodles and toppings.

Garnish:
- Garnish with chopped scallions, fresh herbs, bean sprouts, crushed peanuts, lime wedges, and chili flakes (if desired).

Serve:
- Serve Mi Quang hot, allowing everyone to mix the ingredients and savor the rich flavors of this Quang style noodle dish.

Enjoy:
- Enjoy the unique and delicious taste of Mi Quang, a specialty from the Quang Nam Province in Central Vietnam!

# Bun Thit Nuong Cha Gio (Grilled Pork Noodles with Spring Rolls)

*Ingredients:*

*For the Grilled Pork:*

- 1 lb (450g) pork shoulder or pork loin, thinly sliced
- 3 tablespoons soy sauce
- 2 tablespoons fish sauce
- 2 tablespoons honey or sugar
- 3 cloves garlic, minced
- 1 tablespoon vegetable oil
- Freshly ground black pepper, to taste

*For the Spring Rolls (Cha Gio):*

- 8-10 spring roll wrappers (rice paper)
- 1/2 lb (225g) ground pork
- 1 cup mung bean vermicelli, soaked in hot water and drained
- 1 cup shredded carrots
- 1 cup shredded cabbage
- 2 cloves garlic, minced
- 2 tablespoons fish sauce
- 1 tablespoon soy sauce
- 1 tablespoon vegetable oil
- Freshly ground black pepper, to taste

*For the Noodle Bowl (Bun Thit Nuong):*

- Rice vermicelli noodles, cooked and cooled
- Lettuce leaves
- Fresh herbs (mint, cilantro)
- Bean sprouts
- Sliced cucumber

*For the Nuoc Cham (Dipping Sauce):*

- 3 tablespoons fish sauce
- 2 tablespoons rice vinegar
- 2 tablespoons sugar

- 1/2 cup water
- 2 cloves garlic, minced
- 1 red chili, thinly sliced (optional)

*Instructions:*

Grilled Pork:

   Marinate Pork:
- In a bowl, mix soy sauce, fish sauce, honey (or sugar), minced garlic, vegetable oil, and black pepper.
- Add sliced pork to the marinade, ensuring it's well-coated. Marinate for at least 30 minutes to 2 hours.

   Grill Pork:
- Preheat grill or grill pan. Grill the marinated pork slices until fully cooked and slightly caramelized. Set aside.

Spring Rolls (Cha Gio):

   Prepare Filling:
- In a pan, heat vegetable oil and sauté minced garlic. Add ground pork and cook until browned.
- Add shredded carrots and cabbage. Cook until vegetables are tender.
- Stir in fish sauce, soy sauce, and black pepper. Add mung bean vermicelli and mix well.

   Assemble Spring Rolls:
- Dip each spring roll wrapper in warm water to soften. Place a portion of the filling along one edge and roll tightly, folding in the sides as you go.

   Deep Fry:
- Heat oil for deep frying. Fry the spring rolls until golden brown and crispy. Drain on paper towels.

Noodle Bowl (Bun Thit Nuong):

   Prepare Ingredients:
- Arrange cooked and cooled rice vermicelli noodles, lettuce leaves, fresh herbs, bean sprouts, and sliced cucumber in individual serving bowls.

   Assemble Bowl:

- Top each bowl with the grilled pork slices and a couple of fried spring rolls.

Nuoc Cham (Dipping Sauce):

Prepare Dipping Sauce:
- In a bowl, combine fish sauce, rice vinegar, sugar, water, minced garlic, and sliced red chili (if using). Stir until sugar dissolves.

Serve:

Drizzle with Nuoc Cham:
- Drizzle the noodle bowls with Nuoc Cham or serve the dipping sauce on the side.

Enjoy:
- Mix the ingredients in the bowl, dip the spring rolls in Nuoc Cham, and enjoy the delightful combination of grilled pork and crispy spring rolls with the fresh noodles and herbs!

**Banh Canh Cua (Crab Noodle Soup)**

*Ingredients:*

*For the Broth:*

- 2 lbs (about 907g) crab bodies and claws, cleaned
- 1 onion, peeled and halved
- 1 thumb-sized ginger, sliced
- 1 tablespoon fish sauce
- Salt, to taste

*For the Crab Cake (Cha Cua):*

- 1/2 lb (about 225g) crabmeat, finely chopped
- 2 cloves garlic, minced
- 1 tablespoon fish sauce
- 1 teaspoon sugar
- 1/2 teaspoon black pepper
- 1 egg
- 2 tablespoons tapioca starch or cornstarch

*For the Noodle Soup:*

- 1 lb (about 454g) banh canh noodles (thick Vietnamese tapioca noodles) or udon noodles
- Green onions, chopped
- Fresh cilantro, chopped
- Bean sprouts
- Lime wedges
- Red chili, sliced (optional)

*Instructions:*

Broth:

    Prepare Crab Broth:

- In a large pot, combine crab bodies, onion, ginger, fish sauce, and enough water to cover the crab. Bring to a boil and then simmer for about 1-1.5 hours.
- Strain the broth, discarding solids. Season the broth with salt to taste.

Crab Cake (Cha Cua):

Prepare Crab Cake:
- In a bowl, mix crabmeat, minced garlic, fish sauce, sugar, black pepper, egg, and tapioca starch until well combined.
- Form small crab cakes and set them aside.

Cook Crab Cake:
- In a pan, heat oil over medium heat. Fry the crab cakes until golden brown on both sides. Set aside.

Noodle Soup:

Prepare Noodles:
- Cook banh canh noodles or udon noodles according to package instructions. Drain and set aside.

Assemble Soup:
- In individual bowls, place a portion of noodles.

Add Toppings:
- Top the noodles with a few pieces of crab cake, chopped green onions, cilantro, and bean sprouts.

Pour Broth:
- Ladle the hot crab broth over the noodles and toppings.

Serve:
- Serve Banh Canh Cua hot, garnished with lime wedges and sliced red chili if desired.

Enjoy:
- Savor the rich and flavorful Banh Canh Cua, relishing the combination of tender crab, aromatic broth, and hearty noodles!

**Ca Kho To (Braised Fish in Clay Pot)**

*Ingredients:*

- 2 cups crab meat (picked from cooked crabs)
- 1 lb (450g) tapioca or rice flour noodles (banh canh)
- 6 cups crab or seafood broth
- 1 onion, finely chopped
- 3 cloves garlic, minced
- 2 tablespoons fish sauce
- 1 tablespoon sugar
- 1 teaspoon black pepper
- 1 tablespoon vegetable oil
- Fresh herbs (cilantro, mint)
- Bean sprouts
- Lime wedges
- Red chili, sliced (optional)

*Instructions:*

Prepare Crab Broth:
- Boil crab shells in water to create a flavorful crab broth. Strain and set aside.

Cook Aromatics:
- In a pot, heat vegetable oil. Sauté chopped onions and minced garlic until fragrant.

Add Crab Meat:
- Add crab meat to the pot and stir briefly.

Season:
- Pour in the crab or seafood broth, fish sauce, sugar, and black pepper. Bring to a simmer and let it cook for about 10-15 minutes.

Cook Noodles:
- Cook the tapioca or rice flour noodles according to package instructions. Drain and set aside.

Assemble Soup:
- In individual serving bowls, place a portion of the cooked noodles.

Pour Broth:
- Ladle the crab broth over the noodles and crab meat.

Garnish:

- Garnish the soup with fresh herbs, bean sprouts, lime wedges, and sliced red chili (if using).

Serve:
- Serve Banh Canh Cua hot, allowing the flavors to meld together.

Enjoy:
- Enjoy this comforting and flavorful crab noodle soup, savoring the richness of the crab broth and the tender crab meat!

**Ca Kho To (Braised Fish in Clay Pot)**

*Ingredients:*

- 1 lb (450g) catfish or snakehead fish fillets, cut into chunks
- 3 tablespoons fish sauce
- 2 tablespoons sugar
- 1 tablespoon caramel sauce (optional, for color)
- 2 cloves garlic, minced
- 1 shallot, sliced
- 1 teaspoon black pepper
- 1 tablespoon vegetable oil
- 1 cup coconut water or water
- Green onions and cilantro for garnish

*Instructions:*

Marinate Fish:
- In a bowl, mix fish sauce, sugar, caramel sauce (if using), minced garlic, sliced shallot, and black pepper.
- Add fish chunks to the marinade and let it sit for at least 30 minutes.

Braise Fish:
- In a clay pot or deep skillet, heat vegetable oil over medium heat. Add the marinated fish and cook for a few minutes until the fish starts to brown.

Add Coconut Water:
- Pour coconut water (or water) into the pot, ensuring the fish is submerged. Bring to a simmer.

Simmer:
- Reduce heat to low, cover, and simmer for about 30-40 minutes, allowing the fish to absorb the flavors and the sauce to thicken.

Garnish:
- Garnish with sliced green onions and cilantro.

Serve:
- Serve Ca Kho To hot with steamed rice.

Enjoy:
- Enjoy this traditional Vietnamese dish with its sweet and savory flavors, perfectly complemented by the tender, braised fish!

Nom Hoa Chuoi (Banana Flower Salad)

*Ingredients:*

- 1 banana flower
- 1 carrot, julienned
- 1/2 cup cooked and shredded chicken or boiled shrimp (optional)
- 1/4 cup roasted peanuts, crushed
- 1/4 cup dried shrimp, soaked and drained (optional)
- 1/4 cup mint leaves, chopped
- 1/4 cup Vietnamese coriander (rau răm), chopped (optional)
- 1/4 cup fried shallots
- 1 red chili, sliced (optional)

*For the Dressing:*

- 2 tablespoons fish sauce
- 2 tablespoons lime juice
- 1 tablespoon sugar
- 1 clove garlic, minced
- 1 teaspoon soy sauce (optional)
- 1 teaspoon sesame oil (optional)

*Instructions:*

Prepare Banana Flower:
- Peel and discard the outer layers of the banana flower until you reach the tender, pale layers. Finely slice or julienne the banana flower and soak it in water with a bit of lime or vinegar to prevent browning.

Blanch Banana Flower:
- Bring a pot of water to a boil. Blanch the julienned banana flower for about 3 minutes to soften it. Drain and rinse under cold water.

Prepare Dressing:
- In a small bowl, whisk together fish sauce, lime juice, sugar, minced garlic, soy sauce, and sesame oil until the sugar dissolves.

Assemble Salad:
- In a large bowl, combine the blanched banana flower, julienned carrot, shredded chicken or boiled shrimp (if using), crushed peanuts, soaked dried shrimp (if using), chopped mint leaves, Vietnamese coriander (if using), and fried shallots.

**Toss with Dressing:**
- Pour the dressing over the salad and toss everything together until well combined.

**Garnish:**
- Garnish the salad with sliced red chili (if using).

**Chill:**
- Allow the salad to chill in the refrigerator for about 30 minutes to let the flavors meld.

**Serve:**
- Serve Nom Hoa Chuoi as a refreshing and vibrant side dish or a light meal on its own.

**Enjoy:**
- Enjoy the unique flavors and textures of this delicious Banana Flower Salad, appreciating the combination of crisp banana flower, crunchy vegetables, and the zesty dressing!

## Canh Chua Ca (Sour Fish Soup)

*Ingredients:*

- 1 lb (450g) catfish or snakehead fish fillets, cut into chunks
- 4 cups tamarind water (made by soaking tamarind pulp in warm water and straining)
- 1 liter water or fish stock
- 1 cup bean sprouts
- 1 cup okra, sliced
- 1 medium tomato, sliced
- 1 medium pineapple, peeled and sliced
- 1 long green chili, sliced
- 2 tablespoons fish sauce
- 1 tablespoon sugar
- 1 teaspoon salt
- 1 tablespoon vegetable oil
- Fresh herbs (cilantro, Vietnamese mint)
- Rice or rice noodles, cooked (optional, for serving)

*Instructions:*

Prepare Tamarind Water:
- Soak tamarind pulp in warm water, then strain to extract tamarind water.

Marinate Fish:
- In a bowl, marinate fish chunks with fish sauce for about 15-20 minutes.

Sauté Fish:
- Heat vegetable oil in a pot. Sauté the marinated fish until slightly browned.

Add Tamarind Water:
- Pour in the tamarind water and water or fish stock. Bring to a boil.

Add Vegetables:
- Add sliced okra, tomato, pineapple, and green chili to the pot. Simmer until the vegetables are tender.

Season:
- Season the soup with fish sauce, sugar, and salt. Adjust the seasoning to your taste.

Simmer:

- Let the soup simmer for about 10-15 minutes, allowing the flavors to meld together.

Add Bean Sprouts:
- Just before serving, add bean sprouts to the soup.

Garnish:
- Garnish the Canh Chua with fresh herbs like cilantro and Vietnamese mint.

Serve:
- Serve the soup hot over rice or rice noodles if desired.

Enjoy:
- Enjoy the tangy and savory flavors of Canh Chua Ca, a delicious and comforting Vietnamese sour fish soup!

# Cha Ca Thang Long (Hanoi Turmeric Fish with Dill)

*Ingredients:*

- 1 lb (450g) firm white fish fillets (such as catfish or cod), cut into chunks
- 3 tablespoons fish sauce
- 1 tablespoon turmeric powder
- 1 tablespoon sugar
- 2 tablespoons vegetable oil
- 3 cloves garlic, minced
- 1 tablespoon ginger, minced
- 1 onion, thinly sliced
- 2 green onions, chopped
- 1 cup fresh dill, chopped
- 1 cup fresh basil leaves
- 1 cup peanuts, roasted and crushed
- Rice vermicelli or rice noodles, cooked according to package instructions

*For the Dipping Sauce:*

- 2 tablespoons fish sauce
- 1 tablespoon rice vinegar
- 1 tablespoon sugar
- 1/2 cup water
- 1 clove garlic, minced
- 1 red chili, thinly sliced (optional)

*Instructions:*

Marinate and Cook Fish:

  Marinate Fish:
  - In a bowl, combine fish sauce, turmeric powder, sugar, and vegetable oil. Add fish chunks, ensuring they are well-coated. Marinate for at least 30 minutes.
  
  Cook Fish:
  - Heat a skillet or pan over medium-high heat. Cook the marinated fish chunks until they are fully cooked and slightly caramelized. Set aside.

Prepare Dipping Sauce:

**Mix Dipping Sauce:**
- In a small bowl, mix fish sauce, rice vinegar, sugar, water, minced garlic, and sliced red chili (if using). Stir until the sugar dissolves.

**Stir-Fry Aromatics:**

**Sauté Aromatics:**
- In the same skillet or pan, sauté minced garlic, minced ginger, and sliced onions until aromatic and softened.

**Assemble Cha Ca Thang Long:**

**Combine Ingredients:**
- Add the cooked fish back into the pan with sautéed aromatics. Toss to combine.

**Add Green Onions and Dill:**
- Add chopped green onions and fresh dill to the pan. Toss until well mixed.

**Serve:**
- Serve Cha Ca Thang Long hot over a bed of rice vermicelli or rice noodles.

**Garnish and Enjoy:**

**Garnish:**
- Garnish the dish with fresh basil leaves and crushed peanuts.

**Dipping Sauce:**
- Serve with the prepared dipping sauce on the side.

**Enjoy:**
- Enjoy this iconic Hanoi dish, savoring the aromatic turmeric-infused fish and the fragrant dill, accompanied by the delicious dipping sauce!

## Bun Rieu Cua (Crab Noodle Soup)

*Ingredients:*

*For the Crab Cake:*

- 1 lb (450g) fresh crab meat
- 1 cup shrimp, peeled and deveined
- 1 egg
- 2 tablespoons fish sauce
- 1 teaspoon salt
- 1 teaspoon sugar
- 1/2 cup minced pork (optional)
- 2 tablespoons crab paste or shrimp paste
- 1 cup diced tomatoes
- 1 cup diced tofu (optional)

*For the Soup Base:*

- 1 onion, finely chopped
- 3 cloves garlic, minced
- 1 tablespoon vegetable oil
- 2 liters crab or chicken stock
- 2 tablespoons tomato paste
- 1 tablespoon fish sauce
- 1 teaspoon sugar
- 1 teaspoon salt
- 1 tablespoon tamarind paste or tamarind concentrate
- 1 tablespoon annatto oil (optional, for color)

*For Serving:*

- Rice vermicelli noodles, cooked
- Fresh herbs (mint, cilantro)
- Bean sprouts
- Lime wedges
- Red chili, sliced (optional)

*Instructions:*

Prepare the Crab Cake:

- Mix Ingredients:
  - In a large bowl, combine fresh crab meat, shrimp, egg, fish sauce, salt, sugar, minced pork (if using), crab paste or shrimp paste, diced tomatoes, and diced tofu.
- Blend:
  - Use a food processor or blender to blend the mixture until it becomes a smooth paste.
- Shape Crab Cake:
  - Form the mixture into small crab cakes or patties.
- Cook Crab Cake:
  - Steam the crab cakes for about 15-20 minutes or until cooked through.

Prepare the Soup Base:

- Sauté Aromatics:
  - In a pot, heat vegetable oil and sauté chopped onions and minced garlic until fragrant.
- Add Tomato Paste:
  - Add tomato paste and cook for a few minutes until the color deepens.
- Pour in Stock:
  - Pour in the crab or chicken stock and bring to a simmer.
- Season:
  - Season the soup with fish sauce, sugar, salt, tamarind paste, and annatto oil (if using). Adjust seasoning to taste.

Assemble Bun Rieu Cua:

- Add Crab Cakes:
  - Gently drop the steamed crab cakes into the simmering soup.
- Serve:
  - Serve the Bun Rieu Cua hot over rice vermicelli noodles.

Garnish and Enjoy:

Garnish:
- Garnish the soup with fresh herbs, bean sprouts, lime wedges, and sliced red chili (if using).

Enjoy:
- Enjoy this delightful Crab Noodle Soup, appreciating the rich flavors of the crab cake and the savory-tangy broth!

**Xoi Xeo (Sticky Rice with Mung Beans and Fried Shallots)**

*Ingredients:*

- 2 cups glutinous rice
- 1 cup mung beans, soaked overnight
- 1 cup coconut milk
- 1 teaspoon salt
- 1/2 cup fried shallots (for topping)
- Banana leaves (for wrapping, optional)

*For Garnish (Optional):*

- Shredded coconut, toasted
- Sesame seeds, toasted
- Crushed peanuts

*Instructions:*

Prepare Sticky Rice and Mung Beans:

- Rinse and Soak:
  - Rinse the glutinous rice under cold water until the water runs clear. Soak the rice in water for at least 4 hours or overnight.
- Steam Mung Beans:
  - Steam the soaked mung beans until they are soft, which usually takes about 15-20 minutes.
- Steam Sticky Rice:
  - Drain the soaked glutinous rice. Place it in a steamer lined with cheesecloth or a clean kitchen towel. Steam for about 30-40 minutes or until the rice is tender.
- Combine Rice and Mung Beans:
  - In a large mixing bowl, combine the steamed sticky rice and mung beans. Mix well.

Prepare Coconut Mixture:

Heat Coconut Milk:
- In a saucepan, heat coconut milk over low heat. Add salt and stir until the salt dissolves.

Combine Coconut Mixture:
- Pour the heated coconut milk over the sticky rice and mung beans. Mix thoroughly until the coconut milk is well incorporated.

Assemble Xoi Xeo:

Wrap in Banana Leaves (Optional):
- If using banana leaves, cut them into square pieces. Place a portion of the sticky rice mixture onto each banana leaf square and shape it into a rectangle or square. Fold the sides of the banana leaf over the rice, creating a neat package.

Top with Fried Shallots:
- Sprinkle a generous amount of fried shallots over the top of each portion.

Garnish and Serve:

Optional Garnishes:
- Garnish with toasted shredded coconut, sesame seeds, and crushed peanuts if desired.

Serve Warm:
- Serve Xoi Xeo warm as a delightful snack or breakfast option.

Note: Xoi Xeo is often enjoyed on its own, but you can also pair it with savory dishes, such as grilled meats or pickled vegetables, for a more substantial meal.

## Banh Trang Nuong (Grilled Rice Paper with Toppings)

*Ingredients:*

- 2 cups glutinous rice
- 1 cup split mung beans
- 1/2 cup fried shallots
- 1/4 cup vegetable oil
- 1 teaspoon salt
- 1 tablespoon sugar
- Sesame seeds for garnish (optional)
- Shredded coconut for garnish (optional)
- Banana leaves for serving (optional)

*Instructions:*

Prepare Sticky Rice:
- Rinse the glutinous rice under cold water until the water runs clear. Soak the rice in water for at least 4 hours or overnight.

Steam Mung Beans:
- Rinse the split mung beans and steam them until they are soft. Mash the steamed mung beans into a coarse paste.

Cook Sticky Rice:
- Drain the soaked glutinous rice. In a steamer, steam the glutinous rice for about 20-25 minutes or until fully cooked.

Mix Rice and Mung Beans:
- In a large bowl, combine the steamed glutinous rice and mashed mung beans. Mix well.

Season:
- Add vegetable oil, salt, and sugar to the rice and mung bean mixture. Mix thoroughly.

Shape and Serve:
- Optionally, shape the sticky rice mixture into a round or rectangular cake. Serve on a plate or banana leaves.

Garnish:
- Sprinkle fried shallots on top of the sticky rice. Optionally, garnish with sesame seeds and shredded coconut.

Serve Warm or Cold:

- Xoi Xeo can be served warm or cold. If serving cold, let it cool and firm up before cutting into slices.

Enjoy:

- Enjoy Xoi Xeo as a delightful and satisfying treat, savoring the combination of sticky rice, mung beans, and the savory crunch of fried shallots!

**Banh Trang Nuong (Grilled Rice Paper with Toppings)**

*Ingredients:*

- Rice paper sheets (banh trang)
- Shrimp, cooked and sliced in half (optional)
- Pork belly, thinly sliced and cooked (optional)
- Green onions, chopped
- Roasted peanuts, crushed
- Vietnamese pork floss (bi), optional
- Hoisin sauce
- Sriracha or chili sauce (optional)

*Instructions:*

Preheat Oven or Grill:
- Preheat your oven or grill to medium-high heat.

Prepare Rice Paper:
- Moisten the rice paper sheets with a damp cloth or by quickly dipping them in water. Be careful not to oversoak; they should still be slightly firm.

Add Toppings:
- Place desired toppings on one half of the moistened rice paper. You can include shrimp, pork belly, chopped green onions, crushed peanuts, and pork floss.

Fold and Grill:
- Fold the rice paper over the toppings to create a half-moon shape. Press the edges to seal. Grill the stuffed rice paper on the preheated oven or grill for a few minutes until it becomes crispy.

Serve:
- Serve Banh Trang Nuong hot off the grill, with hoisin sauce and Sriracha on the side for dipping.

Enjoy:
- Enjoy the crispy and flavorful Banh Trang Nuong, relishing the combination of grilled rice paper and delicious toppings!

**Che Ba Mau (Three-Color Dessert)**

*Ingredients:*

For the Mung Bean Layer:

- 1/2 cup split mung beans
- 1/4 cup sugar
- Water for boiling

For the Jelly Layer:

- 1 packet agar-agar powder (or agar-agar strands)
- 1/2 cup sugar
- 4 cups water

For the Coconut Layer:

- 1 can (400ml) coconut milk
- 1/4 cup sugar
- A pinch of salt

For Assembling:

- Crushed ice
- Sweetened red beans (canned or homemade)
- Tapioca pearls, cooked (optional)
- Grass jelly, cubed (optional)

*Instructions:*

Mung Bean Layer:

   Cook Mung Beans:
   - Rinse the split mung beans and cook them in water until soft. Drain any excess water.

Sweeten Mung Beans:
- Mash the cooked mung beans and mix in sugar while they are still warm. Set aside.

Jelly Layer:

Prepare Agar-Agar:
- If using agar-agar strands, soak them in water for about 15-20 minutes. If using agar-agar powder, skip this step.

Boil Agar-Agar:
- In a pot, combine agar-agar, sugar, and water. Bring to a boil, then simmer until the agar-agar is fully dissolved. Let it cool and set aside.

Coconut Layer:

Sweeten Coconut Milk:
- In a separate pot, heat coconut milk, sugar, and a pinch of salt. Stir until the sugar is fully dissolved. Set aside to cool.

Assembling Che Ba Mau:

Prepare Serving Glasses:
- Place a layer of crushed ice in serving glasses or bowls.

Layer Ingredients:
- Spoon a layer of sweetened mung beans over the crushed ice, followed by the agar-agar jelly layer, and then the sweetened coconut milk layer.

Optional Toppings:
- Add sweetened red beans, cooked tapioca pearls, or cubed grass jelly on top as desired.

Serve:
- Serve Che Ba Mau immediately, allowing the layers to meld together.

Enjoy:
- Enjoy this refreshing and colorful Three-Color Dessert, relishing the combination of textures and flavors in each spoonful!

**Bun Bo Hue (Spicy Beef Noodle Soup)**

*Ingredients:*

*For the Mung Bean Layer:*

- 1 cup split mung beans
- 1/2 cup sugar
- Water for boiling

*For the Coconut Milk Layer:*

- 1 can (14 oz) coconut milk
- 1/2 cup sugar
- A pinch of salt

*For the Tapioca Pearl Layer:*

- 1/2 cup small tapioca pearls
- Water for boiling
- 1-2 drops of food coloring (red or green)

*For Serving:*

- Crushed ice
- Coconut water (optional)

*Instructions:*

Prepare Mung Bean Layer:

    Soak Mung Beans:
- Rinse the split mung beans and soak them in water for at least 2 hours or overnight.

    Boil Mung Beans:

- Boil the soaked mung beans until they become soft. Drain any excess water.

Blend Mung Beans:
- Blend the boiled mung beans with sugar until you achieve a smooth paste.

Prepare Coconut Milk Layer:

Mix Coconut Milk:
- In a saucepan, mix coconut milk, sugar, and a pinch of salt. Heat the mixture until the sugar dissolves. Let it cool.

Prepare Tapioca Pearl Layer:

Boil Tapioca Pearls:
- Boil tapioca pearls according to the package instructions. Add food coloring (red or green) to the boiling water to color the pearls. Drain and rinse under cold water.

Assemble Che Ba Mau:

Layering:
- In serving glasses or bowls, layer the blended mung beans, colored tapioca pearls, and coconut milk mixture.

Repeat Layers:
- Repeat the layers until the glasses or bowls are filled.

Chill:
- Refrigerate the Che Ba Mau for at least 1-2 hours to let it set and chill.

Serve:
- Before serving, add crushed ice on top. Optionally, you can pour coconut water over the dessert.

Enjoy:
- Enjoy the refreshing and visually appealing Che Ba Mau with its distinct layers and delightful combination of flavors!

## Bun Bo Hue (Spicy Beef Noodle Soup)

*Ingredients:*

*For the Broth:*

- 2 lbs beef shank or oxtail
- 1 lb beef brisket
- 1 lb pork hocks or pork bones
- 1 onion, halved
- 1 knob ginger, sliced
- 3 lemongrass stalks, bruised
- 3-4 dried chili peppers
- 3 tablespoons annatto seeds (optional, for color)
- 2 tablespoons shrimp paste (optional)
- 2 tablespoons fish sauce
- 1 tablespoon sugar
- Salt, to taste

*For the Hue-Style Vermicelli Bowl:*

- Rice vermicelli noodles, cooked
- Thinly sliced beef (from the beef shank or brisket)
- Pork blood pudding (gio lua huyet), sliced (optional)
- Pork sausage (gio lua), sliced
- Fresh herbs (cilantro, mint, Vietnamese basil)
- Bean sprouts
- Lime wedges
- Chili sauce or sliced red chilies

*Instructions:*

Prepare Broth:

    Parboil Meat:

- Bring a pot of water to a boil. Add beef shank or oxtail, brisket, and pork hocks or bones. Boil for 10 minutes, then discard the water.

Boil Broth:
- In a large pot, add fresh water, parboiled meats, onion, ginger, lemongrass, dried chili peppers, annatto seeds (if using), and shrimp paste (if using). Bring to a boil and then reduce heat to simmer.

Season Broth:
- Add fish sauce, sugar, and salt to the broth. Simmer for at least 1-2 hours until the meats are tender.

Prepare Hue-Style Vermicelli Bowl:

Slice Meats:
- Thinly slice the beef from the shank or brisket. Slice the pork blood pudding and pork sausage.

Assemble Bowl:
- In serving bowls, place cooked rice vermicelli noodles, sliced beef, pork blood pudding, and pork sausage.

Ladle Broth:
- Ladle the hot broth over the ingredients in each bowl.

Garnish:
- Garnish the bowl with fresh herbs, bean sprouts, lime wedges, and chili sauce or sliced red chilies.

Serve:
- Serve Bun Bo Hue hot, allowing diners to mix and match the garnishes according to their preference.

Enjoy:
- Enjoy this robust and flavorful Vietnamese spicy beef noodle soup, savoring the depth of the broth and the variety of textures from the meats and noodles!

**Ca Phe Sua Da (Vietnamese Iced Coffee)**

*Ingredients:*

- 2 tablespoons coarsely ground Vietnamese coffee (preferably Robusta)
- 2 tablespoons sweetened condensed milk
- Ice cubes

*Equipment:*

- Vietnamese drip coffee maker (phin)
- Glass or cup
- Spoon

*Instructions:*

Prepare the Vietnamese Drip Coffee Maker (Phin):
- Place the coffee filter over the glass or cup. Add the coarsely ground coffee into the filter.

Compact Coffee:
- Gently press down on the coffee grounds with the phin's press to compact them.

Brew Coffee:
- Pour a small amount of hot water (about 1-2 tablespoons) over the coffee grounds to moisten them. Allow it to bloom for about 15-20 seconds.

Add Hot Water:
- Fill the phin with hot water, allowing the coffee to drip through. This process may take a few minutes.

Mix Sweetened Condensed Milk:
- While the coffee is dripping, add sweetened condensed milk to a glass. Adjust the amount to your desired sweetness.

Stir Condensed Milk:
- Stir the sweetened condensed milk well to ensure it's smooth and incorporated.

Complete Dripping Process:
- Once the coffee has finished dripping, stir it briefly.

Pour Coffee Over Ice:
- Fill a glass with ice cubes and pour the brewed coffee over the ice.

Mix and Enjoy:

- Stir the coffee and condensed milk together. Adjust the sweetness by adding more condensed milk if needed.

Serve:
- Ca Phe Sua Da is now ready to be served. Enjoy this refreshing Vietnamese iced coffee!

Note: Adjust the coffee-to-condensed milk ratio according to your taste preferences. You can also add more or less ice depending on how strong or diluted you prefer your coffee.

**Nem Nuong Cuon (Grilled Pork Spring Rolls)**

*Ingredients:*

*For the Grilled Pork Patties (Nem Nuong):*

- 1 lb (450g) ground pork
- 2 tablespoons sugar
- 1 tablespoon fish sauce
- 1 tablespoon soy sauce
- 1 tablespoon cornstarch
- 1 teaspoon baking powder
- 2 cloves garlic, minced
- 1 green onion, finely chopped
- Freshly ground black pepper, to taste

*For the Spring Rolls (Cuon):*

- Rice paper wrappers (banh trang)
- Lettuce leaves
- Fresh herbs (mint, cilantro, Thai basil)
- Rice vermicelli noodles, cooked and cooled
- Cucumber, julienned
- Carrots, julienned
- Bean sprouts

*For the Dipping Sauce:*

- 3 tablespoons hoisin sauce
- 2 tablespoons peanut butter
- 1 tablespoon soy sauce
- 1 tablespoon water
- 1 teaspoon sesame oil (optional)
- Crushed peanuts for garnish (optional)

*Instructions:*

Prepare Grilled Pork Patties (Nem Nuong):

    Mix Ingredients:

- In a bowl, combine ground pork, sugar, fish sauce, soy sauce, cornstarch, baking powder, minced garlic, chopped green onion, and black pepper. Mix well.

Form Patties:
- Form small, oval-shaped patties with the pork mixture.

Grill Patties:
- Grill the pork patties on a barbecue or stovetop grill pan until fully cooked and slightly caramelized. Set aside.

Prepare Dipping Sauce:

Mix Dipping Sauce:
- In a small bowl, whisk together hoisin sauce, peanut butter, soy sauce, water, and sesame oil (if using) until well combined. Set aside.

Assemble Nem Nuong Cuon:

Prepare Ingredients:
- Arrange lettuce leaves, fresh herbs, cooked rice vermicelli noodles, julienned cucumber, julienned carrots, bean sprouts, and grilled pork patties in separate bowls.

Soak Rice Paper Wrappers:
- Dip each rice paper wrapper in warm water for a few seconds until pliable.

Assemble Spring Rolls:
- Lay the soaked rice paper on a clean surface. Add a lettuce leaf, a portion of rice vermicelli noodles, herbs, cucumber, carrots, bean sprouts, and a grilled pork patty.

Roll Spring Rolls:
- Fold in the sides and roll tightly to encase the ingredients. Repeat for each spring roll.

Serve:

Slice and Arrange:
- Slice the Nem Nuong Cuon in half and arrange on a serving plate.

Garnish and Serve:
- Optionally, garnish with crushed peanuts and serve with the prepared dipping sauce.

Enjoy:

- Enjoy these delicious Grilled Pork Spring Rolls, dipping them in the flavorful sauce for an extra burst of taste!

**Chao Long (Rice Porridge with Pork Offal)**

*Ingredients:*

*For the Rice Porridge (Chao):*

- 1 cup jasmine rice, washed and drained
- 8 cups chicken or pork broth
- 1 teaspoon salt

*For the Pork Offal:*

- 1 lb (450g) pork liver, thinly sliced
- 1 lb (450g) pork heart, thinly sliced
- 1 lb (450g) pork kidneys, cleaned and thinly sliced
- 1 lb (450g) pork stomach, cleaned and thinly sliced (optional)
- 1 lb (450g) pork intestine, cleaned and thinly sliced (optional)

*For the Accompaniments:*

- Fresh herbs (cilantro, mint, Thai basil)
- Bean sprouts
- Lime wedges
- Sliced red chilies
- Sliced green onions
- Fried shallots
- Shrimp paste (mam tom) or fish sauce for dipping

*Instructions:*

Prepare Rice Porridge:

   Cook Rice:
   - In a large pot, combine the washed jasmine rice and chicken or pork broth. Bring to a boil, then reduce heat to low, cover, and simmer until the rice breaks down and becomes porridge-like. Stir occasionally to prevent sticking.

### Season Porridge:
- Season the rice porridge with salt, adjusting to taste.

## Prepare Pork Offal:

### Clean and Slice Offal:
- Clean the pork offal thoroughly. Slice the pork liver, heart, kidneys, stomach, and intestine into thin pieces.

### Blanch Offal:
- Blanch the pork offal in hot water for a few minutes until they are cooked but still tender. Drain and set aside.

## Assemble Chao Long:

### Serve Porridge:
- Ladle the hot rice porridge into serving bowls.

### Add Pork Offal:
- Arrange a variety of pork offal slices on top of the porridge in each bowl.

## Serve with Accompaniments:

### Garnish:
- Garnish the Chao Long with fresh herbs, bean sprouts, lime wedges, sliced red chilies, sliced green onions, and fried shallots.

### Serve Dipping Sauce:
- Serve shrimp paste (mam tom) or fish sauce on the side for dipping.

### Enjoy:
- Enjoy Chao Long, savoring the rich flavors of the rice porridge and the assortment of pork offal, along with the fresh and aromatic accompaniments!

**Banh Da Lon (Pandan Layer Cake)**

*Ingredients:*

*For the Green Layer:*

- 1 1/4 cups rice flour
- 1/2 cup tapioca starch
- 1 3/4 cups coconut milk
- 1 cup water
- 3/4 cup granulated sugar
- 1/2 teaspoon pandan extract (or more for color and flavor)

*For the Yellow Layer:*

- 1/2 cup rice flour
- 1/4 cup tapioca starch
- 1 1/2 cups coconut milk
- 1/2 cup water
- 1/2 cup granulated sugar
- 1/4 teaspoon turmeric powder (for color)

*For the Mung Bean Filling:*

- 1 cup peeled and split mung beans
- 1/4 cup sugar
- 1/4 cup coconut milk
- 1/4 teaspoon salt

*For the Coconut Layer:*

- 1 1/2 cups coconut cream
- 1/4 teaspoon salt

*Instructions:*

Prepare Mung Bean Filling:

Cook Mung Beans:
- Rinse mung beans and cook them in water until soft. Drain and mash the beans.

Add Sugar and Coconut Milk:
- In a pan, combine mashed mung beans, sugar, and coconut milk. Cook over low heat until the mixture thickens. Set aside.

## Prepare Green and Yellow Layers:

Mix Batter:
- In separate bowls, mix the ingredients for the green and yellow layers. Whisk until there are no lumps.

Cook Layers:
- Pour a thin layer of the green batter into a greased and lined square pan. Steam for 5-7 minutes until the layer sets. Repeat the process with the yellow batter.

Alternate Layers:
- Continue layering the green and yellow batters until all the batter is used. Steam each layer until set before adding the next.

## Assemble Banh Da Lon:

Layer Mung Bean Filling:
- Once the last layer is added, spread the cooked mung bean filling evenly on top.

Finish with Coconut Layer:
- Mix coconut cream with salt and pour it over the mung bean layer. Steam for an additional 15-20 minutes until fully set.

## Serve:

Cool and Cut:
- Allow Banh Da Lon to cool completely before slicing it into squares or diamonds.

Serve and Enjoy:
- Serve Banh Da Lon as a delightful and colorful Vietnamese pandan layer cake, enjoying the unique flavors and textures of each layer!

**Goi Du Du Kho Bo (Green Papaya Salad with Beef Jerky)**

*Ingredients:*

*For the Salad:*

- 1 medium green papaya, peeled and julienned
- 1 carrot, peeled and julienned
- 1/2 cup beef jerky, shredded
- 1/2 cup roasted peanuts, crushed
- 1/4 cup fresh herbs (cilantro, mint, Thai basil), chopped
- 1/4 cup fried shallots

*For the Dressing:*

- 2 tablespoons fish sauce
- 2 tablespoons lime juice
- 1 tablespoon sugar
- 1 clove garlic, minced
- 1 red chili, minced (optional)

*Instructions:*

Prepare Green Papaya and Carrot:
- Peel and julienne the green papaya and carrot. You can use a julienne peeler or a knife to achieve thin strips.

Shred Beef Jerky:
- Shred the beef jerky into thin strips.

Prepare Dressing:
- In a small bowl, whisk together fish sauce, lime juice, sugar, minced garlic, and minced red chili (if using). Adjust the taste according to your preference.

Assemble Salad:
- In a large bowl, combine the julienned green papaya, carrot, shredded beef jerky, crushed roasted peanuts, chopped fresh herbs, and fried shallots.

Toss with Dressing:

- Pour the dressing over the salad and toss everything together until well combined.

Chill:
- Allow the salad to chill in the refrigerator for about 30 minutes to let the flavors meld.

Serve:
- Serve Goi Du Du Kho Bo as a refreshing and flavorful salad. Optionally, garnish with additional peanuts, herbs, and fried shallots.

Enjoy:
- Enjoy the vibrant and delicious Green Papaya Salad with Beef Jerky, savoring the crunchiness of the papaya, the savory beef jerky, and the zesty dressing!

**Mien Ga (Chicken Glass Noodle Soup)**

*Ingredients:*

*For the Chicken Broth:*

- 1 whole chicken (about 3-4 lbs), cleaned and trimmed
- 1 onion, halved
- 1 knob ginger, sliced
- 1-2 teaspoons salt, to taste
- 1 teaspoon sugar
- 1-2 tablespoons fish sauce, to taste
- Water

*For the Glass Noodle Soup:*

- 100g glass noodles (mien), soaked in hot water until softened
- Shredded cooked chicken meat from the broth
- 1 cup wood ear mushrooms, soaked and sliced
- 1 cup shredded cabbage
- 2-3 green onions, finely chopped
- Fresh cilantro and Vietnamese coriander (rau ram) for garnish
- Lime wedges
- Red chili slices (optional)

*For the Dipping Sauce:*

- 2 tablespoons fish sauce
- 1 tablespoon lime juice
- 1 teaspoon sugar
- 1 clove garlic, minced
- Red chili slices (optional)

*Instructions:*

Prepare Chicken Broth:

Boil Chicken:
- In a large pot, bring water to a boil. Add the whole chicken, onion, ginger, salt, sugar, and fish sauce. Reduce heat and simmer for about 45 minutes to 1 hour until the chicken is cooked through.

Remove Chicken:
- Remove the chicken from the pot and shred the meat once it's cool enough to handle. Set aside.

Strain Broth:
- Strain the broth to remove any impurities, onion, and ginger. Adjust the seasoning with more salt and fish sauce if needed.

Prepare Glass Noodle Soup:

Cook Glass Noodles:
- Cook the soaked glass noodles in boiling water for about 2-3 minutes or until tender. Drain and set aside.

Prepare Vegetables:
- In the serving bowls, arrange shredded cabbage, wood ear mushrooms, and a portion of shredded chicken.

Add Glass Noodles:
- Place a handful of cooked glass noodles over the vegetables and chicken in each bowl.

Pour Hot Broth:
- Pour the hot chicken broth over the noodles and ingredients in each bowl.

Prepare Dipping Sauce:

Mix Dipping Sauce:
- In a small bowl, mix fish sauce, lime juice, sugar, minced garlic, and red chili slices (if using). Adjust to taste.

Garnish and Serve:

Garnish with Herbs:
- Garnish the Mien Ga with chopped green onions, fresh cilantro, and Vietnamese coriander (rau ram).

Serve with Lime and Dipping Sauce:

- Serve the soup hot with lime wedges and the prepared dipping sauce on the side.

Enjoy:
- Enjoy the comforting and flavorful Mien Ga, savoring the delicate glass noodles, tender chicken, and aromatic broth!

## Xoi Man (Sweet Sticky Rice with Toppings)

*Ingredients:*

*For the Sweet Sticky Rice Base:*

- 2 cups glutinous rice
- 1 cup coconut milk
- 1/2 cup sugar
- 1/2 teaspoon salt
- Banana leaves for serving (optional)

*For the Toppings:*

- Shredded coconut, steamed
- Mung beans, cooked and mashed
- Roasted sesame seeds
- Crushed peanuts
- Sliced jackfruit or banana
- Coconut sauce (Nuoc Cot Dua)

*Instructions:*

Prepare Sweet Sticky Rice Base:

    Soak Rice:
- Rinse the glutinous rice under cold water until the water runs clear. Soak the rice in water for at least 4 hours or overnight.

    Steam Rice:
- Drain the soaked glutinous rice and steam it until fully cooked. While steaming, mix coconut milk, sugar, and salt. Add this mixture to the cooked rice, mixing well.

    Continue Steaming:
- Continue steaming the rice with the coconut milk mixture for an additional 15-20 minutes until the rice becomes sticky and has absorbed the liquid.

Prepare Toppings:

Shredded Coconut:
- Steam shredded coconut until it's soft and cooked.

Mung Beans:
- Cook mung beans until soft, then mash them into a paste.

Assemble Xoi Man:

Serve on Banana Leaves (Optional):
- If using banana leaves, cut them into squares, heat over an open flame to soften, and shape them into bowls. Alternatively, you can serve the sticky rice on regular plates or bowls.

Layer Sticky Rice:
- Layer the sweet sticky rice on the banana leaves or plates.

Add Toppings:
- Top the sticky rice with steamed shredded coconut, mashed mung beans, roasted sesame seeds, crushed peanuts, and sliced jackfruit or banana.

Drizzle with Coconut Sauce:
- Drizzle the coconut sauce over the toppings.

Garnish:
- Garnish with additional sesame seeds or crushed peanuts if desired.

Serve:
- Serve Xoi Man as a delightful sweet treat, enjoying the combination of flavors and textures.

Enjoy:
- Enjoy the deliciousness of Xoi Man, a traditional Vietnamese sweet sticky rice dish!

# Cha Tom (Grilled Shrimp on Sugar Cane)

*Ingredients:*

- 1 lb (450g) shrimp, peeled and deveined
- 1/2 lb (225g) ground pork
- 2 cloves garlic, minced
- 1 shallot, minced
- 1 tablespoon fish sauce
- 1 teaspoon sugar
- 1/2 teaspoon black pepper
- 1 tablespoon cornstarch
- 1 tablespoon vegetable oil
- Sugar cane sticks, peeled and cut into 4-inch lengths
- Rice vermicelli noodles, cooked (optional)
- Lettuce leaves, herbs (mint, cilantro), and rice paper for wrapping
- Dipping sauce (Nuoc Cham) for serving

*Instructions:*

Prepare Shrimp Mixture:
- In a bowl, combine peeled and deveined shrimp, ground pork, minced garlic, minced shallot, fish sauce, sugar, black pepper, cornstarch, and vegetable oil. Mix well until the ingredients are evenly distributed.

Process the Mixture:
- Transfer the shrimp mixture to a food processor and blend until it becomes a smooth paste.

Shape on Sugar Cane Sticks:
- Take a small portion of the shrimp mixture and shape it onto the end of a sugar cane stick. Repeat for the remaining mixture.

Grill Cha Tom:
- Grill the shrimp and pork mixture on sugar cane sticks over medium-high heat until cooked through and slightly caramelized.

Prepare Rice Vermicelli (Optional):
- If desired, cook rice vermicelli noodles according to package instructions.

Assemble Wraps:
- Arrange lettuce leaves, herbs, rice vermicelli (if using), and Cha Tom on a plate. Place a bowl of warm water on the side for softening rice paper.

Soften Rice Paper:

- Dip each rice paper wrapper into the warm water for a few seconds until pliable. Place it on a clean surface.

Assemble Rolls:
- Place a lettuce leaf on the rice paper, add herbs, rice vermicelli, and a Cha Tom skewer. Fold the sides of the rice paper over the filling, then tightly roll it up, similar to a burrito.

Serve with Dipping Sauce:
- Serve Cha Tom rolls with Nuoc Cham (dipping sauce) on the side.

Enjoy:
- Enjoy Cha Tom as a flavorful and aromatic dish, savoring the grilled shrimp on sugar cane along with the freshness of herbs and the dipping sauce!

**Nom Oi (Pomelo Salad)**

*Ingredients:*

- 1 large pomelo, peeled and segmented
- 1 cup cooked and shredded chicken breast (optional)
- 1 cup cooked shrimp, peeled and deveined
- 1 cup bean sprouts
- 1/2 cup roasted peanuts, crushed
- 1/4 cup fried shallots
- 1/4 cup fresh mint leaves, chopped
- 1/4 cup fresh cilantro leaves, chopped

*For the Dressing:*

- 3 tablespoons fish sauce
- 2 tablespoons lime juice
- 1 tablespoon sugar
- 1 clove garlic, minced
- 1 red chili, minced (optional)

*Instructions:*

Prepare Pomelo:
- Peel the pomelo and separate it into individual segments. Remove any membrane and break the segments into bite-sized pieces.

Cook Chicken and Shrimp:
- If using chicken, cook and shred it. Cook the shrimp and peel them, leaving them whole or cutting them into bite-sized pieces.

Prepare Dressing:
- In a small bowl, whisk together fish sauce, lime juice, sugar, minced garlic, and minced red chili (if using). Adjust the taste to your preference.

Assemble Salad:
- In a large mixing bowl, combine the pomelo segments, shredded chicken (if using), cooked shrimp, bean sprouts, crushed peanuts, fried shallots, chopped mint leaves, and chopped cilantro.

Toss with Dressing:
- Pour the dressing over the salad ingredients and toss everything together until well coated.

Serve:
- Transfer the Nom Oi to a serving platter or individual plates.

Garnish:
- Optionally, garnish the salad with extra crushed peanuts, fried shallots, and fresh herbs.

Enjoy:
- Enjoy this refreshing and vibrant Pomelo Salad, appreciating the combination of sweet pomelo, savory chicken and shrimp, and the zesty dressing!

## Bun Oc (Snail Noodle Soup)

Ingredients:

Snails: Choose fresh, cleaned snails. You can find them in some Asian markets or specialty stores.

Noodles: Rice vermicelli noodles (bun) are commonly used in this dish. Cook them according to the package instructions and set aside.

Broth:
- 1 onion, sliced
- 1 tablespoon vegetable oil
- 1.5 liters (6 cups) chicken or pork broth
- 1-2 lemongrass stalks, bruised
- 2-3 tablespoons fish sauce
- 1 tablespoon sugar
- Salt and pepper to taste

Herbs and Vegetables:
- Fresh herbs such as mint, basil, and cilantro
- Bean sprouts
- Lime wedges
- Red chilies, sliced

Accompaniments:
- Shrimp paste (mam ruoc) or fermented shrimp sauce (nuoc mam ruoc)
- Garlic vinegar sauce (optional)

Instructions:

Prepare the Snails:
- If you have live snails, clean them thoroughly by soaking in water with salt and flour for a few hours. Rinse them well.
- If you're using pre-cleaned snails, rinse them under cold water.

Cook the Broth:
- In a large pot, sauté sliced onions in vegetable oil until fragrant.
- Add chicken or pork broth, lemongrass, fish sauce, sugar, salt, and pepper. Bring to a boil and let it simmer for about 15-20 minutes to infuse the flavors.
- Add the cleaned snails to the broth and cook until they are tender.

Prepare the Accompaniments:

- Mix shrimp paste or fermented shrimp sauce with a bit of water to create a sauce. Adjust the consistency to your liking.
- If using, prepare a garlic vinegar sauce by mixing minced garlic with vinegar.

Assemble the Dish:
- In serving bowls, place a handful of cooked rice vermicelli noodles.
- Ladle the hot broth and snails over the noodles.
- Serve with fresh herbs, bean sprouts, lime wedges, and sliced chilies on the side.

Enjoy:
- Add the shrimp paste or fermented shrimp sauce to your liking, and optionally drizzle with the garlic vinegar sauce.
- Mix well and enjoy your Bun Oc!

This dish offers a unique and delicious experience, combining the tender texture of snails with the vibrant flavors of Vietnamese herbs and spices. Adjust the seasonings to suit your taste preferences.

## Hu Tieu Nam Vang (Cambodian-Style Noodle Soup)

Ingredients:

Broth:

- 1 tablespoon vegetable oil
- 1 onion, chopped
- 3 cloves garlic, minced
- 1 kg (about 2 pounds) pork bones or pork neck bones
- 1 kg (about 2 pounds) chicken bones
- 4-5 liters (16-20 cups) water
- 1-2 tablespoons rock sugar or granulated sugar
- 2-3 tablespoons fish sauce
- Salt and white pepper to taste

Toppings:

- 300g (about 10 ounces) pork loin, thinly sliced
- 300g (about 10 ounces) shrimp, peeled and deveined
- 200g (about 7 ounces) squid, cleaned and sliced into rings
- 200g (about 7 ounces) ground pork
- 200g (about 7 ounces) peeled and deveined shrimp for wontons
- Wonton wrappers
- 200g (about 7 ounces) minced garlic chives or Chinese chives
- 500g (about 1 pound) thin rice noodles (Hu Tieu noodles), soaked in hot water until soft

Garnishes:

- Bean sprouts
- Fresh herbs (cilantro, basil, mint)
- Lime wedges
- Chili slices
- Fried shallots

Instructions:

Prepare the Broth:
- In a large pot, heat vegetable oil and sauté chopped onions and minced garlic until fragrant.
- Add pork bones and chicken bones, and brown them for a few minutes.
- Pour water into the pot and bring to a boil. Skim off any impurities that rise to the surface.
- Add sugar, fish sauce, salt, and white pepper. Reduce the heat to simmer and let it cook for at least 1-2 hours to develop flavors.

Prepare the Toppings:
- For the wontons, mix ground pork, minced garlic chives, salt, and pepper. Place a small amount of the mixture in the center of each wonton wrapper, wet the edges, and fold into a triangle. Press the edges to seal.
- Boil the wontons in a separate pot of boiling water until they float to the surface. Drain and set aside.

Assemble the Dish:
- Cook the Hu Tieu noodles according to the package instructions. Drain and set aside.
- In a pan, quickly cook the pork slices, shrimp, squid, and minced pork. Season with salt and pepper.

Serve:
- In individual bowls, place a portion of cooked noodles.
- Arrange the cooked meats, wontons, and fresh herbs on top of the noodles.
- Ladle the hot broth over the toppings.

Garnish and Enjoy:
- Serve Hu Tieu Nam Vang hot, garnished with bean sprouts, lime wedges, chili slices, and fried shallots.
- Allow diners to customize their bowls with additional fish sauce, soy sauce, or chili sauce according to their taste preferences.

This Hu Tieu Nam Vang recipe offers a delicious and comforting noodle soup with a variety of textures and flavors. Adjust the toppings and seasonings to suit your preferences.

## Goi Ngo Sen (Lotus Stem Salad)

Ingredients:

For the Salad:

　　250g lotus stems, peeled and thinly sliced
　　1 carrot, julienned or shredded
　　1 cucumber, julienned or thinly sliced
　　1 bell pepper (red or yellow), thinly sliced
　　1 small daikon radish, julienned (optional)
　　1 cup cooked and shredded chicken or prawns (optional)
　　1/2 cup roasted peanuts, crushed
　　Fresh herbs (mint, cilantro, basil), chopped

For the Dressing:

　　3 tablespoons fish sauce
　　2 tablespoons rice vinegar
　　1 tablespoon sugar
　　1 clove garlic, minced
　　1 red chili, finely chopped (adjust according to your spice preference)
　　1 tablespoon lime juice

Instructions:

Prepare the Lotus Stems:
- Peel the lotus stems and slice them thinly. If they are tough, blanch them in boiling water for 2-3 minutes to soften slightly. Drain and set aside.

Prepare the Vegetables:
- Julienne or thinly slice the carrot, cucumber, bell pepper, and daikon radish. If using, cook and shred the chicken or prawns.

Make the Dressing:
- In a small bowl, mix together fish sauce, rice vinegar, sugar, minced garlic, chopped red chili, and lime juice. Stir until the sugar dissolves.

Assemble the Salad:
- In a large mixing bowl, combine the prepared lotus stems, vegetables, shredded chicken or prawns (if using), and chopped herbs.

Add the Dressing:

- Pour the dressing over the salad and toss everything together until well combined. Ensure that the dressing coats all the ingredients evenly.

Garnish:
- Sprinkle crushed roasted peanuts over the salad for added crunch.

Chill and Serve:
- Refrigerate the salad for about 30 minutes before serving to allow the flavors to meld.
- Serve the Goi Ngo Sen chilled, garnished with additional herbs and peanuts if desired.

This Lotus Stem Salad is not only visually appealing but also offers a delightful combination of textures and flavors. Feel free to customize the ingredients and adjust the dressing to suit your taste preferences. Enjoy this light and refreshing Vietnamese dish!

**Chao Tom Cuon (Shrimp Paste on Sugarcane Skewers)**

Ingredients:

For the Shrimp Paste:

>500g raw shrimp, peeled and deveined
>2 cloves garlic, minced
>1 shallot, minced
>1 teaspoon sugar
>1/2 teaspoon salt
>1/4 teaspoon white pepper
>1 tablespoon fish sauce
>1 tablespoon cornstarch
>1 egg white

For the Sugarcane Skewers:

>Sugarcane sticks, peeled and cut into 4-5 inch lengths

For Serving:

>Rice paper sheets
>Lettuce leaves
>Fresh herbs (mint, basil, cilantro)
>Rice vermicelli, cooked according to package instructions
>Dipping sauce (Nuoc Cham)

Instructions:

>Prepare the Shrimp Paste:
>- In a food processor, combine raw shrimp, minced garlic, minced shallot, sugar, salt, white pepper, fish sauce, cornstarch, and egg white.
>- Blend the mixture until you get a smooth paste.
>
>Shape the Shrimp Paste on Sugarcane Skewers:
>- Take a small amount of the shrimp paste and mold it onto a sugarcane stick. The paste should cover about 2-3 inches of the stick. Make sure it's evenly coated.
>- Repeat the process for the remaining sugarcane sticks and shrimp paste.
>
>Grill the Chao Tom:

- Preheat a grill or grill pan over medium heat.
- Grill the shrimp paste on sugarcane skewers for 3-4 minutes on each side or until they are cooked through and have a nice golden color.

Prepare the Accompaniments:
- Soften rice paper sheets by dipping them in warm water for a few seconds until pliable.
- Assemble a plate of lettuce leaves, fresh herbs, and cooked rice vermicelli.

Assemble the Chao Tom Cuon:
- To make a roll, place a softened rice paper sheet on a plate.
- Add a lettuce leaf, a portion of rice vermicelli, and a few fresh herbs.
- Place a grilled Chao Tom on top and roll everything tightly, similar to a spring roll.

Serve with Dipping Sauce:
- Prepare a dipping sauce (Nuoc Cham) with fish sauce, lime juice, sugar, water, and chopped chili. Adjust the quantities to suit your taste.

Enjoy:
- Dip the Chao Tom Cuon in the Nuoc Cham and enjoy the delightful combination of flavors and textures.

Chao Tom Cuon is not only delicious but also a fun and interactive appetizer. The sugarcane skewers impart a subtle sweetness to the shrimp paste, creating a unique and satisfying dish.

**Banh Chung (Traditional Tet Sticky Rice Cake)**

Ingredients:

For the Filling:

- 500g glutinous rice
- 200g split yellow mung beans
- 300g pork belly, cut into small cubes
- 1 teaspoon salt
- 1/2 teaspoon pepper
- 1 tablespoon fish sauce
- 1 tablespoon minced shallots
- 1 tablespoon minced garlic
- Banana leaves (for wrapping)

For Assembly:

- Kitchen twine or banana leaf strips for tying

Instructions:

Prepare the Ingredients:
- Soak the glutinous rice in water for at least 4 hours or overnight. Drain.
- Soak the mung beans in water for about 2 hours. Drain.
- Season the pork belly with salt, pepper, fish sauce, minced shallots, and minced garlic. Mix well and let it marinate for at least 30 minutes.

Assemble the Banh Chung:
- Cut banana leaves into squares large enough to wrap the Banh Chung. You'll need two squares for each Banh Chung.
- Lay two banana leaf squares on top of each other. Place a portion of soaked glutinous rice in the center, spreading it out into a square shape.
- Add a layer of soaked mung beans on top of the rice.
- Place a portion of marinated pork on the mung beans.
- Cover the filling with another layer of soaked mung beans, then another layer of glutinous rice.
- Fold the banana leaves over the filling, creating a square package. Tie the package securely with kitchen twine or banana leaf strips.

Boil the Banh Chung:

- Bring a large pot of water to a boil.
- Immerse the wrapped Banh Chung in the boiling water. Make sure the Banh Chung is fully submerged.
- Boil for about 6-8 hours. You may need to add more water during the boiling process to ensure it stays submerged.

Cool and Serve:
- Once cooked, remove the Banh Chung from the water and let it cool. You can place a heavy object on top to help compress and shape the cake as it cools.
- Once cooled, remove the twine or banana leaf strips.
- Cut the Banh Chung into slices or cubes before serving.

Banh Chung is traditionally enjoyed with pickled onions, Vietnamese pork sausage (gio lua), and sometimes with a sprinkle of ground black pepper. It is a symbolic and cherished dish during Tet, symbolizing prosperity and the earth.

## Bun Mang Vit (Duck and Bamboo Shoot Noodle Soup)

Ingredients:

For the Broth:

- 1 whole duck (about 2-3 pounds), cleaned and chopped into serving pieces
- 1 onion, peeled and halved
- 2-3 slices of ginger
- 1 cinnamon stick
- 2-3 star anise
- 2-3 cloves
- 1 cardamom pod
- 2-3 stalks lemongrass, bruised
- 1-2 tablespoons fish sauce
- Salt and sugar to taste

For the Soup:

- Thin rice vermicelli noodles (bun), cooked according to package instructions
- Bamboo shoots, sliced into thin strips
- Fresh herbs (cilantro, mint, basil)
- Bean sprouts
- Red chilies, sliced
- Lime wedges

Optional Garnishes:

- Fried shallots
- Green onions, chopped

Instructions:

Prepare the Duck:
- Rinse the duck pieces under cold water. If there are any excess fat pockets, you can trim them.
- In a large pot, boil water and blanch the duck pieces for a few minutes. Discard the water.

Make the Broth:

- Fill the pot with clean water.
- Add the blanched duck, halved onion, ginger slices, cinnamon stick, star anise, cloves, cardamom pod, lemongrass, fish sauce, salt, and sugar.
- Bring the pot to a boil, then reduce the heat to simmer. Skim off any impurities that rise to the surface.
- Simmer for at least 1.5 to 2 hours until the duck is tender, and the broth is flavorful.

Prepare the Soup Ingredients:
- While the broth is simmering, prepare the rice vermicelli noodles according to the package instructions.
- Slice bamboo shoots into thin strips.
- Wash and prepare the fresh herbs, bean sprouts, and red chilies.

Assemble the Bun Mang Vit:
- In serving bowls, place a portion of cooked rice vermicelli noodles.
- Add slices of bamboo shoots and a few pieces of cooked duck on top.
- Ladle the hot broth over the noodles and duck.

Garnish and Serve:
- Garnish the Bun Mang Vit with fresh herbs, bean sprouts, sliced red chilies, lime wedges, and optional fried shallots and chopped green onions.

Enjoy:
- Serve the Bun Mang Vit hot, allowing diners to customize their bowls with additional fish sauce, lime juice, or chili according to their taste preferences.

Bun Mang Vit is a hearty and flavorful noodle soup that showcases the rich taste of duck and the earthy flavors of bamboo shoots. It's a comforting dish, especially popular during Tet (Vietnamese Lunar New Year) or on special occasions.

## Xoi Gac (Red Sticky Rice)

Ingredients:

    2 cups glutinous rice
    1 Gac fruit (also known as baby jackfruit or spiny bitter gourd)
    1 cup coconut milk
    1/2 cup sugar
    1/2 teaspoon salt
    Banana leaves for wrapping (optional)

Instructions:

    Prepare the Glutinous Rice:
- Rinse the glutinous rice under cold water until the water runs clear.
- Soak the rice in water for at least 4 hours or overnight.

    Extract Gac Fruit Pulp:
- Cut the Gac fruit in half and scoop out the seeds and bright orange flesh.
- Use a spoon or fork to mash the Gac fruit flesh into a smooth pulp. Strain to remove seeds, if necessary.

    Cook the Rice:
- Drain the soaked glutinous rice and place it in a steamer lined with cheesecloth or a clean kitchen towel.
- Steam the rice over high heat for about 20-25 minutes or until it becomes translucent and sticky.

    Prepare the Coconut Sauce:
- In a saucepan, combine the Gac fruit pulp, coconut milk, sugar, and salt.
- Cook over medium heat, stirring constantly, until the mixture thickens and becomes a smooth sauce. This will take about 10-15 minutes.

    Mix the Sticky Rice and Coconut Sauce:
- Transfer the steamed glutinous rice to a large mixing bowl.
- Pour the Gac fruit and coconut sauce over the rice and gently fold until the rice is evenly coated.

    Wrap in Banana Leaves (Optional):
- If using banana leaves, cut them into square pieces, and quickly pass them over an open flame to make them pliable.
- Place a portion of the sticky rice mixture in the center of a banana leaf square and fold it into a neat package.

    Serve:
- Arrange the Xoi Gac on a serving platter or individual plates.

- Optionally, you can shape the sticky rice into molds or cut it into squares for serving.

Enjoy:
- Serve Xoi Gac warm and enjoy the unique flavor and vibrant color of this traditional Vietnamese dish.

Xoi Gac is not only delicious but also visually appealing, making it a festive addition to any special occasion or celebration. The natural red color from the Gac fruit gives the sticky rice a distinctive and attractive appearance.

**Goi Ca Trich (Jellyfish Salad)**

Ingredients:

For the Salad:

- 200g jellyfish, soaked and shredded (available in Asian grocery stores)
- 1 carrot, julienned
- 1 cucumber, julienned
- 1/2 daikon radish, julienned
- 1 bell pepper (red or yellow), thinly sliced
- 1/2 cup fresh herbs (cilantro, mint, basil), chopped
- 1/4 cup roasted peanuts, crushed
- Sesame seeds (optional)

For the Dressing:

- 3 tablespoons fish sauce
- 2 tablespoons rice vinegar
- 1 tablespoon sugar
- 1 clove garlic, minced
- 1 red chili, finely chopped (adjust according to your spice preference)
- 1 tablespoon lime juice

Instructions:

Prepare the Jellyfish:
- Soak the jellyfish in cold water for a few hours or according to the package instructions to rehydrate.
- Shred the jellyfish into thin strips.

Prepare the Vegetables:
- Julienne the carrot, cucumber, daikon radish, and thinly slice the bell pepper.
- Chop the fresh herbs.

Make the Dressing:
- In a small bowl, mix together fish sauce, rice vinegar, sugar, minced garlic, chopped red chili, and lime juice. Stir until the sugar dissolves.

Assemble the Salad:

- In a large mixing bowl, combine the shredded jellyfish, julienned vegetables, sliced bell pepper, chopped herbs, and crushed roasted peanuts.

Add the Dressing:
- Pour the dressing over the salad and toss everything together until well combined. Ensure that the dressing coats all the ingredients evenly.

Garnish:
- Optionally, sprinkle sesame seeds on top for added flavor and texture.

Chill and Serve:
- Refrigerate the jellyfish salad for about 30 minutes before serving to allow the flavors to meld.

Enjoy:
- Serve Goi Ca Trich chilled, either as a refreshing appetizer or a side dish.

This jellyfish salad offers a unique combination of textures and flavors, with the crispness of vegetables and the chewiness of jellyfish. Adjust the spice level and other ingredients according to your preferences.

**Banh Cuon (Steamed Rice Rolls)**

Ingredients:

For the Rice Rolls:

> 1 cup rice flour
> 1/4 cup tapioca starch
> 2 cups water
> 1/2 teaspoon salt
> Cooking spray or oil for greasing the steamer tray

For the Filling:

> Ground pork
> Wood ear mushrooms, soaked and finely chopped
> Dried shrimp, soaked and finely chopped
> Shallots, finely minced
> Fish sauce, soy sauce, salt, and pepper to taste
> Cooking oil for sautéing

For Serving:

> Fresh herbs (cilantro, mint)
> Bean sprouts
> Vietnamese fish sauce (Nuoc Cham)

Instructions:

Make the Rice Rolls:

> In a bowl, mix rice flour, tapioca starch, water, and salt. Stir well to create a smooth, thin batter.
> Heat a steamer tray and lightly grease it with cooking spray or oil.
> Pour a thin layer of the batter onto the steamer tray, swirling it around to evenly coat the surface. Cover and steam for about 2-3 minutes or until the rice sheet is set.

Carefully lift the steamed rice sheet using a spatula and transfer it to a plate.
Repeat the process until all the batter is used.

## Prepare the Filling:

In a pan, heat cooking oil and sauté minced shallots until fragrant.
Add ground pork and cook until browned. Season with fish sauce, soy sauce, salt, and pepper to taste.
Add chopped wood ear mushrooms and dried shrimp. Cook until the mushrooms are tender.
Adjust the seasonings as needed and set the filling aside.

## Assemble the Banh Cuon:

Lay a steamed rice sheet on a clean surface.
Place a spoonful of the prepared filling in the center of the rice sheet.
Fold the sides of the rice sheet over the filling and roll it up, creating a tight cylinder.
Repeat the process with the remaining rice sheets and filling.

## Serve:

Arrange the rolled Banh Cuon on a plate.
Serve with fresh herbs, bean sprouts, and a side of Vietnamese fish sauce (Nuoc Cham) for dipping.
Optionally, you can garnish with fried shallots and drizzle with a bit of oil before serving.

Banh Cuon is a delicate and delicious dish, often enjoyed as a light breakfast or snack.

The combination of tender rice sheets and savory filling, along with the freshness of herbs and the tangy dipping sauce, makes it a flavorful and satisfying choice.

**Oc Len Xao Dua (Stir-Fried Snails with Coconut Milk)**

Ingredients:

For the Snails:

- 500g live snails, cleaned and purged (you can find them in some Asian markets)
- 1 tablespoon rice wine or white wine
- 1 tablespoon lime or kumquat juice
- Salt for cleaning the snails

For the Coconut Milk Sauce:

- 1 cup coconut milk
- 2 tablespoons vegetable oil
- 2 cloves garlic, minced
- 1 shallot, finely chopped
- 1 lemongrass stalk, bruised and finely chopped
- 1-2 red chili peppers, sliced (adjust according to spice preference)
- 1 tablespoon fish sauce
- 1 tablespoon sugar
- Salt and pepper to taste

For Garnish:

- Fresh herbs (cilantro, mint, basil)
- Lime wedges
- Chopped peanuts (optional)

Instructions:

Prepare the Snails:
- Clean the live snails thoroughly by soaking them in cold water with salt and lime or kumquat juice for a few hours. Rinse them well to remove any impurities.

Make the Coconut Milk Sauce:
- In a pan, heat vegetable oil over medium heat.
- Add minced garlic, chopped shallot, and lemongrass. Sauté until fragrant.
- Add sliced red chili peppers and continue to sauté for another minute.

- Pour in coconut milk, fish sauce, sugar, salt, and pepper. Stir well and let it simmer for a few minutes until the sauce thickens slightly.

Cook the Snails:
- In a separate pot, bring water to a boil. Add the cleaned snails and boil for about 10-15 minutes until they are cooked.
- Drain the snails and add them to the coconut milk sauce. Stir to coat the snails in the sauce.

Serve:
- Transfer the stir-fried snails with coconut milk to a serving plate.
- Garnish with fresh herbs, lime wedges, and chopped peanuts (if using).

Enjoy:
- Serve Oc Len Xao Dua hot as a delicious appetizer or as part of a seafood feast.

This dish provides a unique combination of flavors, with the richness of coconut milk complementing the tender snails. Adjust the seasonings to your taste and enjoy this Vietnamese delicacy!

Nom Hoa Chuoi Xanh (Green Banana Flower Salad)

## Ingredients:

For the Salad:

- 1 green banana flower
- 1 carrot, julienned
- 1/2 cup cooked and shredded chicken (optional)
- 1/4 cup roasted peanuts, crushed
- 1/4 cup dried shrimp, soaked in warm water (optional)
- Fresh herbs (mint, cilantro, basil), chopped

For the Dressing:

- 2 tablespoons fish sauce
- 2 tablespoons rice vinegar
- 1 tablespoon sugar
- 1 clove garlic, minced
- 1-2 red chilies, finely chopped (adjust to taste)

1 tablespoon lime juice

Instructions:

Prepare the Banana Flower:
- Peel away the outer layers of the banana flower until you reach the tender, pale yellow heart.
- Finely shred the banana flower using a sharp knife or a mandoline slicer.
- Soak the shredded banana flower in a bowl of cold water with a little lime or vinegar to prevent discoloration. Let it soak for about 15-20 minutes, then drain.

Prepare the Dressing:
- In a small bowl, mix together fish sauce, rice vinegar, sugar, minced garlic, chopped red chilies, and lime juice. Stir until the sugar dissolves.

Assemble the Salad:
- In a large mixing bowl, combine the shredded banana flower, julienned carrots, shredded chicken (if using), crushed peanuts, soaked dried shrimp (if using), and chopped fresh herbs.

Add the Dressing:
- Pour the dressing over the salad and toss everything together until well coated with the dressing.

Serve:
- Arrange the Green Banana Flower Salad on a serving platter or individual plates.

Garnish:
- Garnish the salad with additional chopped herbs and peanuts if desired.

Enjoy:
- Serve the Nom Hoa Chuoi Xanh immediately, offering a refreshing and flavorful side dish.

This salad offers a unique combination of textures and flavors, with the banana flower providing a crisp and slightly nutty taste. Adjust the dressing to suit your preferences and enjoy this delicious Vietnamese dish!

**Bun Oc (Escargot Noodle Soup)**

Ingredients:

For the Broth:

    500g cleaned snails
    1 onion, sliced
    2-3 cloves garlic, minced
    1 tablespoon vegetable oil
    1.5 liters (6 cups) chicken or pork broth
    1-2 lemongrass stalks, bruised
    2-3 tablespoons fish sauce
    1 tablespoon sugar
    Salt and pepper to taste

For the Toppings:

    Rice vermicelli noodles (bun), cooked according to package instructions
    Fresh herbs (mint, basil, cilantro)
    Bean sprouts
    Lime wedges
    Red chilies, sliced
    Fried shallots (optional)

For the Dipping Sauce:

    2 tablespoons fish sauce
    1 tablespoon lime juice
    1 teaspoon sugar
    1-2 cloves garlic, minced
    Red chili, sliced (optional)

Instructions:

    Prepare the Snails:
- Clean the snails thoroughly, removing any dirt or impurities. Soak them in water with salt and flour for a few hours, then rinse well.

    Cook the Broth:

- In a large pot, sauté sliced onions and minced garlic in vegetable oil until fragrant.
- Add chicken or pork broth, lemongrass, fish sauce, sugar, salt, and pepper. Bring to a boil and let it simmer for about 15-20 minutes to develop flavors.
- Add the cleaned snails to the broth and cook until they are tender.

Prepare the Dipping Sauce:
- In a small bowl, mix fish sauce, lime juice, sugar, minced garlic, and sliced red chili (if using). Set aside.

Assemble the Dish:
- In serving bowls, place a handful of cooked rice vermicelli noodles.
- Ladle the hot broth and snails over the noodles.

Top with Fresh Ingredients:
- Add fresh herbs, bean sprouts, lime wedges, and sliced red chilies on top.

Optional Garnish:
- Sprinkle fried shallots over the bowl for added flavor and crunch.

Serve with Dipping Sauce:
- Serve Bun Oc hot, with the dipping sauce on the side. Diners can customize their bowls by adding the dipping sauce according to their taste.

Bun Oc offers a unique and savory experience with the tender texture of snails combined with the aromatic broth and fresh herbs. Adjust the seasonings and toppings to suit your preferences. Enjoy!

**Che Troi Nuoc (Glutinous Rice Balls in Ginger Syrup)**

Ingredients:

For the Glutinous Rice Balls:

    1 cup glutinous rice flour
    1/4 cup water
    1/2 cup mung bean paste (homemade or store-bought)

For the Ginger Syrup:

    2 cups water
    1 cup sugar
    2-3 slices of ginger (about 2 inches each)

For Garnish (optional):

    Toasted sesame seeds
    Coconut milk

Instructions:

Making the Glutinous Rice Balls:

    In a mixing bowl, combine the glutinous rice flour with water. Knead the mixture until it forms a smooth and elastic dough.
    Pinch off small portions of the dough and roll them into small balls, about 1/2 to 1 inch in diameter.
    Flatten each ball into a small disk and place a small amount of mung bean paste in the center.
    Seal the edges and roll it back into a ball, ensuring that the mung bean paste is completely enclosed.
    Repeat the process until all the glutinous rice balls are filled.

Making the Ginger Syrup:

    In a saucepan, combine water, sugar, and ginger slices. Bring to a boil, stirring until the sugar dissolves.

Simmer the ginger syrup for about 10-15 minutes to allow the ginger flavor to infuse into the syrup.
Remove the ginger slices and set the syrup aside.

Cooking the Glutinous Rice Balls:

Bring a pot of water to a boil.
Drop the filled glutinous rice balls into the boiling water. Cook until they float to the surface, indicating that they are cooked through. This usually takes about 5-7 minutes.
Use a slotted spoon to transfer the cooked rice balls into a bowl of cold water to cool and prevent sticking.

Assembly:

Drain the rice balls and place them in serving bowls.
Pour the ginger syrup over the rice balls.
Optionally, drizzle with coconut milk and sprinkle toasted sesame seeds on top for added flavor and texture.
Serve Che Troi Nuoc warm or chilled.

Enjoy this delightful Vietnamese dessert with its combination of chewy glutinous rice balls, sweet ginger syrup, and creamy coconut milk if desired. Che Troi Nuoc is commonly enjoyed during special occasions and festivals.

**Banh Cam (Orange Sesame Balls)**

Ingredients:

For the Filling:

    1 cup mung bean, peeled and split
    1/2 cup sugar
    1/4 cup coconut milk
    A pinch of salt

For the Dough:

    1 cup glutinous rice flour
    1/4 cup rice flour
    1/4 cup sugar
    1/2 cup water
    1/2 teaspoon baking powder
    Orange food coloring (or natural alternatives like turmeric)

For Coating:

    White sesame seeds

For Frying:

    Vegetable oil for deep frying

Instructions:

Making the Filling:

    Rinse the mung beans under cold water. In a saucepan, combine mung beans with enough water to cover them. Bring to a boil and then simmer until the beans are soft.
    Drain any excess water and mash the cooked mung beans.
    In a pan, combine the mashed mung beans, sugar, coconut milk, and a pinch of salt. Cook over medium heat, stirring continuously, until the mixture thickens. Let it cool.

Form small balls (about 1-inch in diameter) with the mung bean mixture. Set aside.

Making the Dough:

In a mixing bowl, combine glutinous rice flour, rice flour, sugar, and baking powder.
Gradually add water to the dry ingredients and mix until you get a smooth, sticky dough.
Divide the dough into equal portions and add orange food coloring to one portion to achieve the desired color.

Assembly:

Take a piece of the orange dough and flatten it in the palm of your hand.
Place a mung bean ball in the center and encase it with the dough, forming a smooth ball.
Roll the ball in white sesame seeds until coated evenly.

Frying:

Heat vegetable oil in a deep fryer or a heavy-bottomed pan to 350-375°F (175-190°C).
Carefully drop the sesame-coated balls into the hot oil and fry until they turn golden brown and crispy.
Remove the Banh Cam from the oil and drain excess oil on paper towels.
Let them cool slightly before serving.

Enjoy these delightful Banh Cam as a sweet treat with a perfect contrast of crispy and chewy textures. They are often enjoyed during Lunar New Year celebrations and other special occasions.

**Lau Ca Keo (Basa Fish Hot Pot)**

Ingredients:

For the Broth:

2 liters (8 cups) fish or vegetable broth
1 onion, sliced
2-3 tomatoes, sliced
1 pineapple, peeled and sliced
3-4 slices of ginger
3-4 stalks lemongrass, bruised
2 tablespoons fish sauce
1 tablespoon sugar
Salt and pepper to taste

For the Hot Pot:

500g basa fish fillets, cut into bite-sized pieces
200g shrimp, peeled and deveined
200g squid, cleaned and sliced into rings
200g fish cakes, sliced
200g mushrooms, sliced
200g Napa cabbage, sliced
200g water spinach (rau muong) or other leafy greens
1 tofu block, cut into cubes
Rice vermicelli noodles (bun), soaked in hot water until soft
Fresh herbs (cilantro, mint, basil)
Lime wedges
Chili slices

Instructions:

Prepare the Broth:
- In a large pot, bring the fish or vegetable broth to a boil.
- Add sliced onion, tomatoes, pineapple, ginger, lemongrass, fish sauce, sugar, salt, and pepper.
- Reduce the heat to simmer and let it cook for at least 30-45 minutes to allow the flavors to infuse.

Prepare the Ingredients:
- Arrange the basa fish, shrimp, squid, fish cakes, mushrooms, Napa cabbage, water spinach, tofu, and soaked rice vermicelli noodles on a serving platter.

Set Up the Hot Pot:
- Place the hot pot in the center of the table and set up a portable stove.
- Pour the prepared broth into the hot pot and let it simmer.

Enjoy Hot Pot:
- Invite diners to add their chosen ingredients to the hot pot, cooking them in the simmering broth.

Serve:
- Once the ingredients are cooked, use a ladle to scoop the hot pot contents into individual bowls.

Garnish and Accompaniments:
- Garnish the hot pot with fresh herbs, lime wedges, and chili slices.
- Serve with dipping sauces like fish sauce with lime, soy sauce with garlic, or a homemade chili sauce.

Enjoy:
- Enjoy Lau Ca Keo with friends and family, dipping the cooked ingredients into your favorite sauces.

Lau Ca Keo is a delightful and interactive meal, perfect for gatherings and celebrations. Adjust the ingredients and broth seasonings to your taste preferences and enjoy the communal experience of hot pot dining.

**Che Ba Ba (Tapioca and Coconut Milk Dessert)**

Ingredients:

For the Tapioca and Coconut Milk Dessert:

    1 cup small tapioca pearls (bubbles), soaked in water for about 1 hour and drained
    1 cup cooked yellow mung beans
    1 cup sweet potatoes, peeled and diced
    1 cup taro, peeled and diced
    1 cup cassava, peeled and diced
    1 cup coconut milk
    1 cup water
    1 cup sugar (adjust to taste)
    1/4 teaspoon salt

For Garnish (optional):

    Crushed ice
    Sesame seeds
    Toasted coconut flakes

Instructions:

Prepare the Tapioca Pearls:
- Soak the small tapioca pearls in water for about 1 hour or until they become translucent. Drain and set aside.

Cook Mung Beans and Root Vegetables:
- Boil the yellow mung beans until soft. Drain and set aside.
- In separate pots, cook the sweet potatoes, taro, and cassava until they are tender. Drain and set aside.

Prepare Coconut Milk Syrup:
- In a saucepan, combine coconut milk, water, sugar, and salt. Heat over medium heat until the sugar dissolves and the mixture is well combined.

Assemble Che Ba Ba:
- In serving bowls or glasses, layer the soaked tapioca pearls, cooked mung beans, and the boiled sweet potatoes, taro, and cassava.

Pour Coconut Milk Syrup:

- Pour the warm coconut milk syrup over the layers of ingredients in each serving bowl.

Garnish:
- Optionally, garnish with crushed ice, sesame seeds, and toasted coconut flakes.

Serve:
- Serve Che Ba Ba immediately, allowing the dessert to be enjoyed warm or at room temperature.

Enjoy:
- Enjoy the sweet and creamy goodness of Che Ba Ba, savoring the combination of textures and flavors.

This Vietnamese dessert is not only visually appealing with its colorful layers but also offers a delightful mix of tastes and textures. Adjust the sweetness according to your preference and enjoy Che Ba Ba as a refreshing treat, especially on warm days.

**Banh It Tran (Sticky Rice Dumplings)**

Ingredients:

For the Dumplings:

    2 cups glutinous rice flour
    1/2 cup water
    1/4 cup sugar
    1/4 teaspoon salt

For the Filling:

    1 cup mung beans, peeled and soaked for at least 4 hours
    1/2 cup shredded coconut (fresh or desiccated)
    1/2 cup sugar
    1/4 teaspoon salt

For Coating (Optional):

    Grated coconut or toasted sesame seeds

Instructions:

Making the Dumplings:

    In a mixing bowl, combine glutinous rice flour, sugar, and salt.
    Gradually add water to the dry ingredients, stirring continuously until you achieve a smooth and elastic dough.
    Divide the dough into small portions, shaping them into balls. Set aside.

Making the Filling:

    Drain the soaked mung beans and steam them until they are fully cooked and easily mashed.
    In a pan, combine the cooked mung beans, shredded coconut, sugar, and salt. Cook over medium heat, stirring continuously until the mixture thickens and becomes a cohesive filling.
    Let the mung bean filling cool before handling.

Assembling the Dumplings:

Flatten each dough ball into a disc and place a small amount of the mung bean filling in the center.

Enclose the filling by folding and sealing the edges, forming a dumpling. Ensure that the filling is fully covered.

Repeat the process for the remaining dough and filling.

Cooking the Dumplings:

Steam the dumplings over boiling water for about 15-20 minutes or until the dumplings are cooked through.

Optionally, coat the steamed dumplings with grated coconut or toasted sesame seeds.

Serve:

Let the Banh It Tran cool slightly before serving.

Enjoy these delicious sticky rice dumplings as a delightful snack or dessert.

Banh It Tran showcases the harmonious blend of sticky rice, mung bean, and coconut, creating a flavorful and slightly sweet treat. Adjust the sweetness to your liking and savor these delightful dumplings, often enjoyed during various Vietnamese celebrations and family gatherings.

**Bun Mang Vit (Duck and Bamboo Shoot Noodle Soup)**

Ingredients:

For the Duck Broth:

    1 whole duck (about 3-4 pounds), cleaned and cut into serving pieces
    1 onion, peeled and halved
    2-3 slices of ginger
    1 cinnamon stick
    2-3 star anise
    2-3 cloves
    1 cardamom pod
    2-3 stalks lemongrass, bruised
    2-3 tablespoons fish sauce
    Salt and sugar to taste

For the Soup:

    Rice vermicelli noodles (bun), cooked according to package instructions
    Bamboo shoots, sliced into thin strips
    1-2 cups cooked shredded duck meat (from the broth)
    Fresh herbs (cilantro, mint, basil)
    Bean sprouts
    Lime wedges
    Red chilies, sliced

For Garnish:

    Fried shallots
    Green onions, chopped

Instructions:

Making the Duck Broth:

    In a large pot, bring water to a boil. Add the duck pieces and boil for about 5-10 minutes to remove any impurities. Discard the water and clean the duck pieces.

In the same pot, add fresh water, duck pieces, onion, ginger, cinnamon stick, star anise, cloves, cardamom pod, lemongrass, fish sauce, salt, and sugar.

Bring the pot to a boil, then reduce the heat to simmer. Skim off any impurities that rise to the surface. Simmer for at least 1.5 to 2 hours until the duck is tender, and the broth is flavorful.

Remove the duck pieces from the broth, shred the meat, and set it aside.

Assembling the Soup:

In serving bowls, place a portion of cooked rice vermicelli noodles.
Add slices of bamboo shoots and a handful of cooked shredded duck on top.
Ladle the hot duck broth over the noodles and duck.

Garnish and Serve:

Garnish the Bun Mang Vit with fresh herbs, bean sprouts, sliced red chilies, lime wedges, fried shallots, and chopped green onions.

Optionally, serve with a side of fish sauce, lime, and chili for diners to adjust the flavor to their liking.

Enjoy the Bun Mang Vit hot, savoring the rich and aromatic duck broth with tender duck meat and the unique texture of bamboo shoots.

Bun Mang Vit is a comforting and hearty noodle soup, perfect for those who enjoy the rich flavor of duck and the freshness of Vietnamese herbs. Adjust the seasonings and toppings according to your taste preferences.

**Goi Ngo Sen (Lotus Stem Salad)**

Ingredients:

For the Salad:

    1 lotus stem, peeled and thinly sliced
    1 carrot, julienned or shredded
    1 cucumber, julienned or thinly sliced
    1/2 cup cooked and shredded chicken (optional)
    1/4 cup roasted peanuts, crushed
    Fresh herbs (mint, cilantro, basil), chopped
    1 red chili, sliced (optional)

For the Dressing:

    2 tablespoons fish sauce
    2 tablespoons rice vinegar
    1 tablespoon sugar
    1 clove garlic, minced
    1-2 red chilies, finely chopped (adjust to taste)
    1 tablespoon lime juice

Instructions:

Prepare the Lotus Stem:
- Peel the lotus stem and slice it thinly. If the stem is tough, blanch it in boiling water for 2-3 minutes to soften. Drain and set aside.

Prepare the Vegetables:
- Julienne or thinly slice the carrot and cucumber.
- If using chicken, cook and shred it.

Make the Dressing:
- In a small bowl, mix together fish sauce, rice vinegar, sugar, minced garlic, chopped red chilies, and lime juice. Stir until the sugar dissolves.

Assemble the Salad:
- In a large mixing bowl, combine the sliced lotus stem, julienned carrot, sliced cucumber, shredded chicken (if using), crushed peanuts, and chopped fresh herbs.

Add the Dressing:

- Pour the dressing over the salad ingredients. Toss everything together until well coated with the dressing.

Garnish:
- Garnish the salad with additional chopped herbs and sliced red chilies if desired.

Serve:
- Serve Goi Ngo Sen immediately, offering a refreshing and crunchy Vietnamese salad.

Adjust the dressing ingredients according to your taste preferences, and feel free to customize the salad with additional herbs or toppings. Goi Ngo Sen makes for a delightful side dish or a light and healthy meal on its own.

**Cha Ca La Vong (Hanoi Turmeric Fish with Dill)**

Ingredients:

For the Marinade:

- 500g firm white fish fillets (such as catfish or cod), cut into chunks
- 2 tablespoons fish sauce
- 1 tablespoon turmeric powder
- 1 tablespoon minced garlic
- 1 tablespoon minced ginger
- 2 tablespoons vegetable oil
- 1 tablespoon sugar
- Salt and pepper to taste

For Cooking:

- 2 tablespoons vegetable oil
- 1 large onion, thinly sliced
- 1 bunch fresh dill, roughly chopped
- 1 cup roasted peanuts, coarsely crushed
- 1 cup bean sprouts
- 1 bunch spring onions, chopped into 2-inch lengths
- Fresh herbs (coriander, mint, basil)
- Cooked rice vermicelli noodles or rice paper sheets (for serving)

For Serving:

Fish sauce, lime wedges, and sliced red chilies

Instructions:

Marinating the Fish:

In a bowl, combine fish sauce, turmeric powder, minced garlic, minced ginger, vegetable oil, sugar, salt, and pepper to create the marinade.
Add the fish chunks to the marinade, ensuring they are well-coated. Let it marinate for at least 30 minutes to allow the flavors to infuse.

Cooking Cha Ca La Vong:

Heat vegetable oil in a pan over medium heat.

Add the marinated fish chunks to the pan and cook until they are golden brown and cooked through. This usually takes about 5-7 minutes.

In the same pan, add sliced onions and cook until they are soft and caramelized.

Stir in the chopped dill and cook for an additional 2-3 minutes until the dill is wilted.

Assembling:

Transfer the cooked fish, onions, and dill to a serving platter.

Sprinkle roasted crushed peanuts over the top.

Serve Cha Ca La Vong with bean sprouts, chopped spring onions, fresh herbs, and either rice vermicelli noodles or rice paper sheets.

Serving:

To eat, place a portion of Cha Ca La Vong on a plate or rice paper sheet, along with noodles or rice.

Top with fresh herbs, bean sprouts, and chopped spring onions.

Drizzle with fish sauce, squeeze lime wedges, and add sliced red chilies according to taste.

Mix everything together and enjoy the unique flavors of Cha Ca La Vong.

This dish offers a delightful combination of turmeric-infused fish, aromatic dill, and a variety of fresh herbs. Customize the toppings and adjust the seasonings to suit your preferences. Cha Ca La Vong is not just a meal; it's a flavorful and interactive dining experience.

## Muc Nuong Sa Ot (Grilled Lemongrass Squid)

Ingredients:

For the Marinade:

> 500g whole squid or cleaned squid tubes
> 3 stalks lemongrass, finely minced
> 3 cloves garlic, minced
> 2 tablespoons fish sauce
> 1 tablespoon soy sauce
> 1 tablespoon sugar
> 2 tablespoons vegetable oil
> 1 tablespoon oyster sauce
> 1 tablespoon chili paste or minced fresh red chili (adjust to taste)
> Salt and pepper to taste

For Garnish (optional):

> Fresh cilantro or mint
> Lime wedges

Instructions:

- Prepare the Squid:
  - If using whole squid, clean and remove the innards. Score the squid tubes in a crisscross pattern on both sides.
- Make the Marinade:
  - In a bowl, combine lemongrass, minced garlic, fish sauce, soy sauce, sugar, vegetable oil, oyster sauce, chili paste or minced chili, salt, and pepper. Mix well to form a smooth marinade.
- Marinate the Squid:
  - Coat the squid thoroughly with the marinade, ensuring it gets into the scored areas. Allow it to marinate for at least 30 minutes to an hour in the refrigerator.
- Grill the Squid:
  - Preheat a grill or grill pan over medium-high heat.
  - Grill the squid for about 2-3 minutes on each side or until it's cooked through and has a nice char.

Garnish and Serve:
- Transfer the grilled squid to a serving plate.
- Garnish with fresh cilantro or mint and serve with lime wedges on the side.

Enjoy:
- Serve Muc Nuong Sa Ot hot, either as an appetizer or a main dish.

This Grilled Lemongrass Squid is known for its bold and zesty flavors, making it a popular street food and appetizer in Vietnamese cuisine. Adjust the spice level according to your preference, and enjoy the unique combination of lemongrass, chili, and grilled squid.

**Che Bap (Corn Pudding)**

Ingredients:

- 1 cup corn kernels (fresh or frozen)
- 1 cup glutinous rice (sticky rice)
- 1 cup coconut milk
- 1 cup sugar
- 4 cups water
- 1/4 teaspoon salt
- 1 tablespoon cornstarch (optional, for thickening)
- Toasted sesame seeds or roasted peanuts for garnish (optional)

Instructions:

Prepare the Glutinous Rice:
- Rinse the glutinous rice under cold water until the water runs clear.
- Soak the rice in water for at least 4 hours or overnight.

Cook the Glutinous Rice:
- Drain the soaked glutinous rice.
- In a steamer, steam the glutinous rice for about 20-25 minutes or until it becomes tender.

Prepare the Corn Pudding Base:
- In a blender, combine corn kernels, coconut milk, sugar, and water. Blend until you get a smooth mixture.

Cook the Corn Pudding:
- Pour the blended mixture into a pot and bring it to a simmer over medium heat.
- Add salt and continue to cook, stirring frequently, for about 10-15 minutes.

Add the Glutinous Rice:
- Add the steamed glutinous rice to the pot and stir well to combine.
- If you prefer a thicker consistency, mix cornstarch with a bit of water to create a slurry and gradually add it to the pot while stirring.

Simmer and Thicken:
- Allow the mixture to simmer for an additional 10-15 minutes until it thickens to your desired consistency.

Serve:
- Ladle the Che Bap into serving bowls.

Garnish (Optional):
- Garnish with toasted sesame seeds or roasted peanuts if desired.

Enjoy:
- Serve Che Bap warm or chilled, as a delightful and sweet Vietnamese dessert.

Che Bap is not only comforting but also a wonderful way to enjoy the natural sweetness of corn combined with the richness of coconut milk. Adjust the sugar to your liking and savor this delicious dessert.

www.ingramcontent.com/pod-product-compliance
Lightning Source LLC
LaVergne TN
LVHW081555060526
838201LV00054B/1901